Birds of the Algarve
and Southern Alentejo
An Annotated Checklist

Gonçalo Elias

Birds of the Algarve and Southern Alentejo

An Annotated Checklist

Title: Birds of the Algarve: An Annotated Checklist
Author: Gonçalo Elias
Text revision: Thijs Valkenburg
Cover page: Rufous-tailed Scrub Robin *Cercotrichas galactotes*
                 (Pedro Marques)
Production: C. Maria Elias
Printing: Createspace.com
Distribution: Amazon.com

1st edition, March 2016

ISBN: 978-1517497811

Print On Demand

Contact: goncalo.elias@gmail.com

CONTENTS

Introduction

In recent years birdwatching activities have markedly increased in Portugal, as a result of an increasing interest shown by society at large. This interest appears to be the result, on one hand, of a greater awareness being shown towards environmental issues and, on the other hand, of technological innovations, digital photography and the Internet amongst them, which made it easier to obtain and share pictures of the natural world, at low cost.

Thanks to this rapid increase in the number of people interested in birds, the amount of information about birds seen in the wild in Portugal has also risen sharply in the last few years. Because of that, existing references, namely those that deal with bird species occurring in Portugal and with their status in this country, become rapidly outdated.

Birds of the Algarve and Southern Alentejo - An Annotated Checklist has been written with two objectives in mind. Firstly, to provide an update to the existing species lists and secondly, to make this information available in a practical and accessible format that can be easily understood and used by anyone with an interest in birds, including those that belong to the non-specialized public.

The format chosen – an annotated list – is more than just an inventory: for each species mentioned, a brief description is provided about its migratory status, its abundance and its distribution in southern Portugal. For the species that are only irregularly recorded – often referred to as 'rarities' – a brief summary of the existing records is provided.

It is hoped that this list will, in its modest way, contribute to a better understanding of the avifauna of southern Portugal. Also it is to be hoped that it can be used as a basis for any future updates, whenever there is a relevant amount of new information to be added.

Methodology

In order to construct this annotated bird list, all available information concerning birds that have been recorded in the wild in southern Portugal has been consulted. In this section, the criteria used for selecting the information are presented.

Geographical span

This book focuses on the territory of southern Portugal, namely Algarve (Faro district) and southern Alentejo (Beja district) as well as on the adjacent marine areas, which form the territorial waters.

Time span

The list comprises available information about all the birds recorded in the Algarve and southern Alentejo up until the last day of February 2016.

Sources of information

All records that have been published in books, journals and other works were taken into consideration. Additionally, several recent records that have not been published on paper but that were made available via the Internet, namely in specialized sites, blogs and discussion groups, are included.

During the preparation of this list, many relevant works were checked. The most important ones are:

- *Aves de Portugal – Ornitologia do território continental*, for information about movements and distribution;

- *Atlas das Aves Nidificantes em Portugal*, for information about the distribution and abundance of breeding birds;

- *Portuguese Rarities Committee Reports*, for records of rare or vagrant species;

- *Anuário Ornitológico*, for data about the species of uncertain origin, for information about exotic birds and also for records of uncommon species;

- *Aves Exóticas que nidificam em Portugal Continental*, for information about the situation of non-native birds.

A full list of all works checked can be found in the Bibliography section (page 81).

Validation of records

The identification of birds in the wild is not always easy and identification errors occur, often as a result of confusion with other species. In order to clarify the status of birds that turn up away from their normal distribution area, the information referring to rare birds is usually scrutinized by experienced members of a rarities committee. These committees produce reports relating to accepted records of rare birds. In the case of Portugal, this task was accomplished by the Iberian Rarities Committee (Comité Ibérico de Rarezas) between 1987 and 1994 and by the Portuguese Rarities Committee (Comité Português de Raridades or PRC) from 1995 onwards.

The most recent records (especially those of 2011 and onwards) have not yet been included in any reports. However, in most cases, the birds were photographed and the pictures have been published on the Internet, namely in forums, blogs or photography groups; in many cases, the identification of the birds does not raise significant doubt. It is reasonable to presume that these records will be accepted and hence these records have been included in this list.

In the case of records dating from before 1987, the existing documentation is sometimes rather poor; in these cases, relevant published information has been included in the list, mentioning the quality of the existing evidence, where appropriate.

Common Bird Names

Despite all the efforts carried out by different organizations to standardize common bird names, there are many species for which there can be more than one name, as there are extant many different lists of names. This can be a source of confusion.

The common names used in this list are those used by the Association of European Records and Rarities Committees (AERC).

Scientific Bird Names

The systematics of birds has undergone changes in recent years and there are varying arguments about what is the best taxonomic approach. The existing institutions and field guides use different criteria and often this is also a source of confusion for birdwatchers.

In the present list, the sequence and the scientific names follow the recommendations of the Association of European Records and Rarities Committees (AERC).

List presentation

The following list comprises a total of 401 species that have been seen in the wild in southern Portugal.

The information about the species has been grouped as follows:

- Systematic List of Birds: Species that have been recorded in an apparently natural state or which have wild self-sustaining populations – this includes autochthonous species, natural vagrants and exotic species that have naturalized themselves – 392 species.

- Appendix: Species of uncertain origin – species that have been recorded, but for which their putative wild origin raises some doubts or cannot be ascertained – 9 species.

Systematic List of Birds

The list presented in this section comprises a total of 392 species of birds that have been recorded in an apparently natural state or which have wild self-sustaining populations – this includes autochthonous species, natural vagrants and exotic species that have naturalized themselves.

1. Whooper Swan *Cygnus cygnus*

An adult overwintered at Altura, Castro Marim, from November 2009 until February 2010. Initially there were two birds, but one of them died.

2. Bean Goose *Anser fabalis*

A single record is known: one bird was seen at the Faro sewage works in December 1993.

3. Greylag Goose *Anser anser*

A scarce winter visitor, which occurs from November through February. The main wintering site is at Lagoa dos Patos, Alvito, where up to one hundred birds are regularly seen. The species has been occasionally recorded at several other places, usually in very small numbers.

4. Barnacle Goose *Branta leucopsis*

Only three records are known: the first was at the Tavira saltpans, where two birds were seen in December 2010; the second one was at Quinta do Lago, where a singleton overwintered from October 2011 until April 2012; finally, a flock of six turned up at Lagoa dos Patos, Alvito, in December 2014.

5. Brant Goose *Branta bernicla*

A rare winter visitor, which is not recorded every year. About 20 records are known, in some cases involving small flocks. Most sightings took place between October and March, in coastal wetlands. An unusually large number of birds were seen during the 2014-15 winter.

6. Ruddy Shelduck *Tadorna ferruginea*

About 11 records are known from 1990 onwards, with the first four months of the year holding the largest number of sightings. The origin of these birds has been questioned and it is likely that some of them have escaped from captivity.

7. Common Shelduck *Tadorna tadorna*

An uncommon resident, which breeds in very small numbers in the wetlands of the eastern Algarve, namely around Castro Marim and Ria Formosa. Numbers are augmented in winter, presumably by birds originating from other European countries. Only rarely recorded in the southern Alentejo.

8. Eurasian Wigeon *Anas penelope*

A common but rather localised winter visitor, which occurs mainly from September to March, with occasional records from other months. The wintering population is largely concentrated in the Ria Formosa and sometimes exceeds two thousand birds. Smaller numbers occur at other coastal wetlands and also inland.

9. American Wigeon *Anas americana*

Three records are known, all of them referring to single males: one at Lagoa dos Patos, Alvito, in February 1998, another one at the Faro sewage works in November and December 2013 and finally one at the last-named place in January 2015.

10. Gadwall *Anas strepera*

A fairly common resident and probably a wintering species, it breeds in several wetlands along the south coast and also at inland reservoirs.

11. Eurasian Teal *Anas crecca*

An abundant winter visitor, which occurs from September to March. It can be found in most coastal wetlands and also at reservoirs in the Alentejo.

12. Green-winged Teal *Anas carolinensis*

A rare vagrant, which has been recorded on two occasions only: one at Salgados lagoon in February 2010 and another one at the same place in February and March 2011. Both sightings refer to single males.

13. Mallard *Anas platyrhynchos*

A common resident, which can be found throughout the year on any type of wetland. Large numbers concentrate at coastal wetlands during autumn and early winter.

14. Northern Pintail *Anas acuta*

An uncommon winter visitor, which occurs from November to March, with occasional records from other months. Largely concentrated at the main coastal wetlands, particularly in the Ria Formosa area. Quite scarce inland.

15. Garganey *Anas querquedula*

A scarce passage migrant, which turns up regularly from February to May and again from August to October, with scattered records from other months. More conspicuous during pre-nuptial passage, when males show their colourful breeding plumage.

16. Blue-winged Teal *Anas discors*

A rare vagrant, with ten known records, nine of them in the Algarve and the remaining one at Lagoa dos Patos, Alvito. The period of observation spans mid-September to March.

17. Northern Shoveler *Anas clypeata*

A common winter visitor, which occurs mainly from September to April. As with most dabbling ducks, the winter population is largely concentrated in coastal wetlands; small numbers occur inland. There are several spring records and breeding has been proved in the Alentejo and Algarve provinces, in very small numbers.

18. Marbled Duck *Marmaronetta angustirostris*

Two records only: three birds at Ludo, Faro, in January 1988 and another one at the same place in January 1997.

19. Red-crested Pochard *Netta rufina*

An uncommon species which breeds at several places in the Alentejo and also in the Algarve. It can be seen throughout the year.

20. Common Pochard *Aythya ferina*

An uncommon winter visitor, its numbers seem to fluctuate markedly from year to year. It can be found at coastal and inland waters, usually in small numbers, but it can be locally numerous and flocks of many hundred birds are reported on occasion. A few pairs breed in the Alentejo and in the central Algarve.

21. Ring-necked Duck *Aythya collaris*

Eight records are known of this Nearctic vagrant, all between September and April. Records come from coastal wetlands and inland reservoirs. Most of them refer to singletons, but on two occasions two birds were seen together.

22. Ferruginous Duck *Aythya nyroca*

A rare winter visitor, which occurs mainly from October to March, although there are a few records from other months as well. The largest known gatherings involved 47 birds at Vilamoura in autumn 2015, 27 birds at the same place in November 2012 and 18 birds near Ferreira do Alentejo in December 2012. Breeds irregularly in the Algarve.

23. Tufted Duck *Aythya fuligula*

An uncommon winter visitor, seen mainly from October to March. This diving duck turns up at coastal and inland waters, almost always in small numbers, but flocks of one hundred or more are sometimes seen in the Alentejo reservoirs.

24. Greater Scaup *Aythya marila*

A very rare winter visitor, which occurs between October and March at coastal wetlands and, occasionally, on inland reservoirs. Most records involve single birds, although small flocks have been seen at times.

25. Lesser Scaup *Aythya affinis*

An adult male was seen at Salgados lagoon in March 2003. This is the only record.

26. Common Eider *Somateria mollissima*

A very rare vagrant, which has been irregularly reported in late summer, autumn and winter. The few existing records come from coastal wetlands or from the open sea, along the southern coast of the Algarve.

27. Long-tailed Duck *Clangula hyemalis*

Eight records are known of this duck, all made at coastal wetlands in the Algarve. Sightings have been made between November and April.

28. Common Scoter *Melanitta nigra*

A fairly common winter visitor, which occurs mainly in open sea, not far from the coastline. Smaller numbers turn up at coastal wetlands. The main period of occurrence spans from August to April, with occasional sightings at other times of the year.

29. Surf Scoter *Melanitta perspicillata*

Two records only, both in the Algarve: one at the Dunas Douradas beach, Loulé, in December 2009 and another one at Ancão beach, Loulé, in January 2014.

30. Velvet Scoter *Melanitta fusca*

A rare vagrant from northern Europe, which has been recorded in the Algarve on two occasions only: one at Cacela Velha, Vila Real de Santo António, in December 1997 and another one at lagoa do Almargem, Loulé, in January 2014.

31. Bufflehead *Bucephala albeola*

One at Aldeia Nova, Vila Real de Santo António, in January and February 2016.

32. Red-breasted Merganser *Mergus serrator*

A very scarce winter visitor, which occurs mostly between November and March at coastal wetlands. It is very rare inland.

33. Common Merganser *Mergus merganser*

A rare vagrant, with only two known records, both in the Algarve: on at Ria de Alvor in January 2011 and another one at Quarteira, Loulé, in November 2011.

34. Ruddy Duck *Oxyura jamaicensis*

A rare vagrant. Although this duck is native to North America, it has been introduced in the United Kingdom and it is believed that birds seen in Portugal have originated from this introduced population. There are five records in the region, of which four in the Algarve and the other one in the Alentejo province. All records involved single birds and took place between January and April.

35. White-headed Duck *Oxyura leucocephala*

A rare vagrant from the Mediterranean. Nine records are known, all in the Algarve and mostly referring to single birds. More than half of the sightings were made in autumn, the remaining ones at other times of the year.

36. Common Quail *Coturnix coturnix*

A common and widespread breeding species, which is particularly abundant in the Alentejo plains. This species is present in the region throughout the year, but its population is partially migratory.

37. Red-legged Partridge *Alectoris rufa*

A common resident, which can be found throughout the region in open or slightly wooded areas. It is more numerous inland than near the coastline and it is particularly abundant in southeastern Alentejo and northeastern Algarve.

38. Red-throated Loon *Gavia stellata*

A rare vagrant, which has been recorded twice: one was seen at Faro beach in December 2006 and another one was at the Guadiana river mouth in December 2012.

39. Great Northern Loon *Gavia immer*

A rare winter visitor, which has been recorded about 15 times in the last 20 years. Most records come from along the south coast and took place between November and May, with a marked peak in December.

40. Little Grebe *Tachybaptus ruficollis*

A common resident, which can be found throughout the region, although its abundance varies markedly. It is more numerous in the central part of the Alentejo and also at certain places along the southern Algarve coast.

41. Great Crested Grebe *Podiceps cristatus*

An uncommon resident, which favours medium-sized and large reservoirs, mainly in the Alentejo. There is also a small resident population on the Algarve coast.

42. Horned Grebe *Podiceps auritus*

One at Faro harbour in February 2011.

43. Black-necked Grebe *Podiceps nigricolis*

A scarce winter visitor, which favours estuaries and coastal lagoons and occurs mainly from September to April. The Castro Marim reserve is the main wintering site and it can hold up to 100 birds at times. Elsewhere the species turns up in small numbers. Rather rare inland, with odd records at reservoirs in the Alentejo.

44. Northern Fulmar *Fulmarus glacialis*

A rare vagrant, which has been recorded on two occasions only: one was seen at Ponta da Atalaia, Aljezur, in August 1997 and another one was found dead at the Faro beach in January 2010.

45. Cory's Shearwater *Calonectris diomedea*

This seabird can be seen along the entire coast, sometimes in large numbers. The species is usually present from March to November, being rare during winter months.

46. Great Shearwater *Puffinus gravis*

An uncommon passage migrant close to the coast which is, however, quite numerous offshore. It turns up in

Portuguese waters during late summer and early autumn, mainly from mid August to October. Sometimes it is seen from land.

47. Sooty Shearwater *Puffinus griseus*

An uncommon passage migrant, which occurs mostly from August to October. Like the preceding species, it is more abundant offshore. It is regularly seen from land, usually in small numbers, but under certain weather conditions the count may reach several tens per hour.

48. Manx Shearwater *Puffinus puffinus*

An uncommon passage migrant, which has been recorded at different times of the year. Its passage seems to be stronger during late summer and early autumn.

49. Balearic Shearwater *Puffinus mauretanicus*

A non-breeding visitor which can be found year round, with two peaks of abundance: the first in early summer and the second in early autumn. Can regularly be seen from land, often in considerable numbers.

50. Macaronesian Shearwater *Puffinus baroli*

A scarce but probably regular passage migrant, originating from the Macaronesian islands. Rather rare in coastal waters – however, there are several records in July and August in the south Exclusive Economic Zone, where the species is probably regular.

51. Wilson's Storm Petrel *Oceanites oceanicus*

An uncommon passage migrant, which seems to be regular at sea, although it is rarely seen from land. Record dates span from July to October, with a peak during summer months.

52. European Storm Petrel *Hydrobates pelagicus*

A regular passage migrant, rarely seen from land but which may be common offshore. Its occurrence in the area ranges, at least, from May to October.

53. Leach's Storm Petrel *Oceanodroma leucorhoa*

An uncommon winter visitor, seen mainly from October to February. Its appearance near the coast is usually related to the occurrence of storms, when this petrel is often seen by land-based observers flying over the sea or even at coastal wetlands. Additionally, on these occasions, dead birds are sometimes found on beaches or even inland.

54. Swinhoe's Storm Petrel *Oceanodroma monorhis*

One trapped and ringed at Ponta da Almádena, Lagos, in June 1998.

55. Band-rumped Storm Petrel *Oceanodroma castro*

A rare non-breeding visitor. Three records are known at Ponta da Almádena, Lagos, referring to birds trapped during ringing sessions, always in June or July. There is also a record of a bird caught at Sagres harbour after a storm in October 2015. It is not clear whether the species occurs at other times of the year.

56. Brown Booby *Sula leucogaster*

One at Ponta da Piedade, Lagos, in July and August 1996.

57. Northern Gannet *Morus bassanus*

A common passage migrant and winter visitor. Although it can be seen along the coast throughout the year, it is more numerous from October to April.

58. Great Cormorant *Phalacrocorax carbo*

A common winter visitor, which is present mainly from September to March, although small numbers can be seen during spring and summer months. It occurs throughout the region, but is more numerous near the coast than inland.

59. European Shag *Phalacrocorax aristotelis*

An uncommon resident, which breeds in some sectors of rocky coast, both in Alentejo and Algarve. Not usually seen away from these areas.

60. Eurasian Bittern *Botaurus stellaris*

A very rare winter visitor to the region. Has been recorded at several coastal wetlands in the Algarve.

61. Little Bittern *Ixobrychus minutus*

A rare breeding visitor, which favours coastal wetlands, but it can also be locally found inland in the southern Alentejo. It occurs largely from April to September. Small numbers overwinter in the Algarve.

62. Black-crowned Night Heron *Nycticorax nycticorax*

A scarce passage migrant. Formerly bred in the region, however the large colonies that existed in the Guadiana valley up to the 1990s have been abandoned. Occasionally seen in winter.

63. Squacco Heron *Ardeola ralloides*

A rare passage migrant, which is seen yearly, but always in very small numbers. The species has been recorded at various times of the year, mostly in coastal wetland areas. Odd birds have been seen in winter.

64. Cattle Egret *Bubulcus ibis*

A common resident. Breeds colonially, often forming mixed colonies with other herons.

65. Western Reef Heron *Egretta gularis*

A rare vagrant, of which only four records are known, all referring to single individuals. Sightings were made between March and May at several coastal locations in the Algarve. Additionally, there are a few records of birds that might be hybrids *E. gularis* x *E. garzetta*.

66. Little Egret *Egretta garzetta*

A common resident, which can often be met with in wetland areas throughout the region, mostly near the coast but also inland. Breeds in colonies, often in association with the Cattle Egret.

67. Great Egret *Egretta alba*

A scarce winter visitor, which can be seen mainly from October to March, although there are a few records in other months. Up to the 1990s this species was very rare in Portugal, but in recent years it has gradually become more frequent and nowadays it can be considered regular in certain areas of the Alentejo. It is, however, a scarce bird in the Algarve.

68. Grey Heron *Ardea cinerea*

Uncommon as a breeding species but numerous as a winter visitor and on migration. Can be found all over the region, in any kind of wetland. It is particularly numerous in coastal wetlands. Breeds isolated or in colonies in the Alentejo.

69. Purple Heron *Ardea purpurea*

An uncommon summer visitor, which breeds in coastal wetlands in central Algarve. Quite rare inland. Usually arrives in March and departs in September, with very few records in other months.

70. Black Stork *Ciconia nigra*

A rare summer visitor, which occurs mostly in the eastern half of the Alentejo. Birds on passage can also be found near the coast, particularly in the Algarve. The species usually arrives in March and departs in September or October, however a few birds remain in the area throughout the winter.

71. White Stork *Ciconia ciconia*

A partial migrant, which occurs throughout the region. It is very numerous in the southern Alentejo, where over 2800 pairs breed. The Algarve breeding population comprises about 400 pairs. A part of the population, mainly young birds, moves to Africa during late summer, but many birds remain in the area throughout the year.

72. Glossy Ibis *Plegadis falcinellus*

An uncommon non-breeding visitor. It can be found in region throughout the year, but it is clearly more numerous during autumn and winter months, particularly at coastal wetlands. Usually seen in small numbers, but flocks of up to 600 have been recorded in the Algarve. There have been breeding records in recent years.

73. Eurasian Spoonbill *Platalea leucorodia*

A rare and localised breeding species, of which there are a few colonies, both in the Alentejo and in the Algarve. Its breeding population seems to be expanding and new colonies have been found in recent years. It is also an uncommon passage migrant and winter visitor, which occurs regularly in most coastal wetlands and, occasionally, in inland waters. Sometimes flocks of up to a few hundred birds are recorded, especially in the Algarve.

74. Greater Flamingo *Phoenicopterus roseus*

A non-breeding visitor that can be seen throughout the year, mainly at coastal wetlands in the Algarve. Occasionally seen at reservoirs in the Alentejo. Although it is generally uncommon, it can be locally abundant, mainly in the Castro Marim reserve, where gatherings of over 1500 have been recorded. Isolated breeding attempts are known to have occurred in the Algarve.

75. European Honey Buzzard *Pernis apivorus*

An uncommon passage migrant, which is regularly seen during the post-nuptial passage, especially in September, at Cape St. Vincent and sometimes elsewhere along the coast. A few pairs may breed in southern Alentejo. Its main period of occurrence spans from April to October.

76. Black-winged Kite *Elanus caeruleus*

An uncommon resident, which is more numerous in the open Alentejo plains, namely around Beja, than elsewhere. However, it seems to be expanding and there are recent breeding records from the Algarve and also from the Alentejo coast. Communal roosts with up to 30 birds have been recorded.

77. Black Kite *Milvus migrans*

A common summer visitor, which is widespread in the Alentejo. The first birds are usually seen in late February or early March, while most departures take place in August. However, there are a few records outside this period, even in midwinter. In the Algarve it is mainly a passage migrant, with very few records during the breeding season.

78. Red Kite *Milvus milvus*

An uncommon winter visitor, which appears mainly between October and March, mostly in the Alentejo, with occasional sightings in the Algarve. Roosts with hundreds of birds exist in the Castro Verde area.

79. Egyptian Vulture *Neophron percnopterus*

A very scarce passage migrant. Formerly bred in southern Alentejo, but this is no longer the case, although odd birds are sometimes seen there during the breeding season. Can be seen on migration in the Algarve, particularly at Cape St. Vincent, where it is regular during post-nuptial passage.

80. Griffon Vulture *Gyps fulvus*

An uncommon resident, which occurs throughout the year over the eastern half of the Alentejo, although it does not breed in the region. In autumn, these vultures turn up regularly in the western Algarve, where flocks of several hundred birds have been reported on several occasions, mostly between mid-October and mid-November.

81. Rüppell's Vulture *Gyps rueppellii*

About 25 records are known, most of them referring to single birds, but there are two records involving three individuals seen together. Sightings come from two distinct areas: the south-eastern part of the Alentejo, not far from the Guadiana valley, and the western Algarve, around Cape St. Vincent. Most records took place between April and November.

82. Cinereous Vulture *Aegypius monachus*

A rare resident, which can be found throughout the year. It is regular along the Spanish border in the Alentejo, but it is much scarcer as one moves westwards and only occasionally is it seen near the coast. After a prolonged absence of several decades as a breeding bird, in 2015 the Cinereous Vulture bred again in the Alentejo, near Moura.

83. Short-toed Snake Eagle *Circaetus gallicus*

An uncommon summer migrant, which occurs throughout the region. It can be seen mainly from March to September, however there are several winter records, most of them in the Algarve.

84. Western Marsh Harrier *Circus aeruginosus*

An uncommon resident and winter visitor, it occurs mainly in coastal wetlands and breeds locally. Additionally, in recent years, this harrier was found breeding in cereal fields in the southern Alentejo.

85. Northern Harrier *Circus cyaneus*

An uncommon winter visitor, which can be seen throughout the area, usually in small numbers. Its main period of occurrence spans from September to March, with odd records at other times of the year.

86. Pallid Harrier *Circus macrourus*

Since 2011 there have been several sightings of this harrier in the Alentejo and Algarve provinces. These were the first ever records of this species in Portugal.

87. Montagu's Harrier *Circus pygargus*

A fairly common summer migrant, which breeds mainly in the open plains of southern Alentejo, with the highest densities around Castro Verde. A few pairs also breed in the eastern Algarve. It is usually present from March to September.

88. Northern Goshawk *Accipiter gentilis*

A very scarce resident, passage migrant and winter visitor. Regularly seen around Cape St. Vincent on autumn migration.

89. Eurasian Sparrowhawk *Accipiter nisus*

An uncommon passage migrant and winter visitor, which may also breed locally in very small numbers. Quite numerous during autumn passage around Cape St. Vincent.

90. Common Buzzard *Buteo buteo*

A common and widespread resident in the Alentejo. In the Algarve it is much less common and breeds mainly inland, whereas in coastal areas it is mostly a non-breeding visitor.

91. Long-legged Buzzard *Buteo rufinus*

Several records, not accepted by the PRC but attributed to this species, have been published, both from the southern

Alentejo and from the Algarve. A few pairs may breed in the Alentejo – this possibility is currently being investigated.

92. Lesser Spotted Eagle *Aquila pomarina*

There are a few isolated records in the Vila do Bispo area, western Algarve, all during the post-nuptial migration, between late September and mid-November.

93. Booted Eagle *Aquila pennata*

An uncommon but widespread summer visitor which can be found over most of southern Alentejo. In the Algarve it is mainly a non-breeding visitor. During migration it can be common in the western Algarve and can often be found in places where it does not breed, particularly at Cape St. Vincent, where several hundred birds pass every autumn. A few individuals remain throughout the winter, mainly around coastal wetlands in the Algarve.

94. Golden Eagle *Aquila chrysaetos*

A rare resident which occurs mainly inland, but its distribution is very discontinuous. Small numbers breed in the eastern Alentejo. Young birds sometimes wander far away from breeding areas.

95. Bonelli's Eagle *Aquila fasciata*

An uncommon resident which is patchily distributed. It occurs mainly in the hilly areas of inner Algarve and also in the forested areas of Alentejo. Wandering immatures sometimes appear far away from breeding areas.

96. Spanish Imperial Eagle *Aquila adalberti*

A rare resident, which was absent for several decades as a breeding species but which has recently recolonized the country. It breeds in small numbers in the southern Alentejo, where its population comprises about six breeding pairs. Juvenile and immature birds are sometimes seen elsewhere, namely in coastal areas.

97. Osprey *Pandion haliaetus*

An uncommon passage migrant and winter visitor. Usually seen close to large water bodies, mainly estuaries, coastal lagoons and reservoirs, therefore it is more frequently seen near the coast. Although it has been recorded at all times of the year, it is more numerous during migration periods. Bred at several locations along the rocky coast up to the end of the 20th century, and a pair bred there again in 2015.

98. Lesser Kestrel *Falco naumanni*

A fairly common breeding visitor, which occurs almost only in the Alentejo. It is usually present between February and August.

99. Common Kestrel *Falco tinnunculus*

A common and widespread resident, which favours open areas, both near the coast and inland.

100. Red-footed Falcon *Falco vespertinus*

A rare passage migrant. Prior to 2015 there were about ten records, either in spring or in autumn. In May 2015 the largest influx on record brought over 100 birds to the country, with many records in the Algarve and also in the Alentejo. The largest flock involved 21 birds near Baleizão, Beja.

101. Merlin *Falco columbarius*

A very scarce winter visitor, which can be seen from October to April. It seems to be more frequent in the Alentejo. Almost always seen isolated, mostly in open areas.

102. Eurasian Hobby *Falco subbuteo*

A very scarce summer visitor and passage migrant. Nowhere common as a breeding bird, but can be regularly seen on passage, especially along the coast. It is present mainly from April to October.

103. Eleonora's Falcon *Falco eleonorae*

An uncommon passage migrant, which has been recorded at various locations, mostly along the coast. Dates of observation range from April to November, with the majority of records in August and September.

104. Lanner Falcon *Falco biarmicus*

This falcon has been recorded on several occasions both in the Algarve and in the Alentejo.

105. Peregrine Falcon *Falco peregrinus*

An uncommon and localised resident and possibly also a winter visitor. During the breeding season it can usually be found around coastal cliffs. At other times of the year it frequently turns up away from breeding areas, namely near wetlands or in open country.

106. Water Rail *Rallus aquaticus*

An uncommon resident, which occurs mainly in coastal wetlands and, locally, in inland waters.

107. Spotted Crake *Porzana porzana*

A rare passage migrant, which may also overwinter. Most records refer to birds seen during the pre-nuptial (February to April) and post-nuptial passage (September to November), but there are also winter records. Most sightings were made in coastal wetland areas; on rare occasions this crake has also been seen inland.

108. Little Crake *Porzana parva*

There are several isolated records of this species, all in the Algarve. Two records were made in 2008 and 2009 during the post-nuptial passage (August and September); the remaining ones were all in 2012 or later, during the pre-nuptial passage (March to May).

109. Baillon's Crake *Porzana pusilla*

May have bred in the past but is currently very rare. Over the last 20 years there have been less than ten records, all referring to singletons, mainly in spring and, occasionally, in autumn and winter.

110. Corn Crake *Crex crex*

One killed at Ingrina, Vila do Bispo, in October 1998. There are also records of birds heard near Ria de Alvor in 1991 and 1995.

111. Common Moorhen *Gallinula chloropus*

A common and widespread resident, which can be seen on any type of wetland.

112. Allen's Gallinule *Porphyrio alleni*

One at Ria de Alvor in April 1990.

113. Purple Swamphen *Porphyrio porphyrio*

An uncommon resident, which occurs in wetland areas. It is more frequent in the Algarve (where it can be locally common) than in the Alentejo, where it is very rare and local.

114. Eurasian Coot *Fulica atra*

A common resident, which occurs mainly in reservoirs and coastal lagoons, sometimes also in fish ponds. It can be locally numerous, with gatherings of hundreds or even thousands of birds having been recorded on several occasions.

115. American Coot *Fulica americana*

One at Ludo, Faro, in September 1992.

116. Red-knobbed Coot *Fulica cristata*

There are at least 24 sightings, most of them in the Algarve, with a few in the Alentejo. Records, usually referring to single birds, have been made at all times of the year, but there are clearly more during autumn and winter months. Some birds were carrying neck-collars, which had been placed as part of a reintroduction program that has been taking place in southern Spain.

117. Common Crane *Grus grus*

An uncommon winter visitor which arrives in late October and leaves in March. It is to be met with almost exclusively in the Alentejo, where there are two main wintering areas: one in the plains between Castro Verde and Beja and the other one around Moura and Barrancos. Very rarely reported elsewhere.

118. Little Bustard *Tetrax tetrax*

An uncommon resident, it occurs mainly in the Alentejo, where it is widespread and locally common. In the Algarve it is scarce and localised. Outside the breeding season it can undertake dispersion movements and sometimes turns up away from breeding areas.

119. Great Bustard *Otis tarda*

An uncommon resident which occurs mainly in the Alentejo, its stronghold being in the Castro Verde plains. Only rarely seen in the Algarve.

120. Eurasian Stone-curlew *Burhinus oedicnemus*

An uncommon but widespread resident, which occurs over most of the Alentejo and also in coastal areas in the Algarve.

121. Black-winged Stilt *Himantopus himantopus*

A common resident, which in the Algarve is chiefly coastal but that in the Alentejo is often found inland. Its migratory pattern is complex, some populations are probably resident, while others are summer migrants and yet some other are passage migrants or possibly winter visitors. Back in 1990 the species wintered in the eastern Algarve only, but its wintering area has expanded since then and currently it also comprises the western Algarve and the Alentejo.

122. Pied Avocet *Recurvirostra avosetta*

An uncommon resident and winter visitor, which occurs mainly on coastal wetlands in central and eastern Algarve, where a small breeding population exists. In the southern Alentejo the Avocet is a very infrequent visitor.

123. Eurasian Oystercatcher *Haematopus ostralegus*

A scarce but regular passage migrant and winter visitor. Almost exclusively found along the coastal strip, being very rare inland. The Ria Formosa, the Ria de Alvor and the Guadiana river mouth are the most important sites for this species. It occurs mainly from August to April, although a few immatures oversummer.

124. Pacific Golden Plover *Pluvialis fulva*

One at Salgados lagoon in July 2007.

125. American Golden Plover *Pluvialis dominica*

A rare vagrant from North America which has been recorded on nine occasions, mostly in autumn. The majority of records were made in the Algarve and the place with the highest number of sightings is the Salgados lagoon. There is also a record from the Alentejo.

126. European Golden Plover *Pluvialis apricaria*

A common winter visitor. It is patchily distributed, although it can be locally numerous especially in the open plains around Castro Verde and Almodôvar. Often associates with flocks of Lapwings. Its main period of occurrence spans from October to February, but there are scattered records of isolated birds or small flocks at other times of the year.

127. Grey Plover *Pluvialis squatarola*

A fairly common non-breeding visitor. It occurs mainly in the large coastal wetlands, where it can be locally numerous at certain times of the year. Can also be seen in small numbers on beaches, but it is very rare inland. Mostly seen in winter and during passage periods; however a few non-breeders can be seen during the breeding season.

128. Sociable Lapwing *Vanellus gregarius*

A rare vagrant, which turns up irregularly during the winter period. About six records are known, from early October to February, all involving single birds.

129. Northern Lapwing *Vanellus vanellus*

A common winter visitor, which can be seen mainly from July to March; it is particularly abundant from October to February, especially in the Alentejo plains. Breeding has been confirmed on several occasions, but these events seem to be sporadic and nowhere regular.

130. Little Ringed Plover *Charadrius dubius*

A widespread summer visitor that is generally uncommon. It occurs mainly from March to September, but there are several winter records.

131. Common Ringed Plover *Charadrius hiaticula*

A common non-breeding visitor, which can be seen in coastal wetlands and sometimes around inland waters. It is numerous during winter and also during passage periods, especially on post-nuptial passage, which peaks in August and September. Several birds remain in the region during the breeding season, but do not breed.

132. Kentish Plover *Charadrius alexandrinus*

A common resident and passage migrant, which can be found along the entire coastline. It can be locally numerous on migration, especially in large wetlands. This plover can also be found in the inner Alentejo in very small numbers.

133. Eurasian Dotterel *Charadrius morinellus*

A regular but very scarce passage migrant, which has been recorded only during the post-nuptial passage and, exceptionally, in winter. The place with the largest number of records is Cape St. Vincent, where the species has been seen almost every year, with small flocks turning up in September and October. Occasionally seen in other places along the coast and, rarely, inland.

134. Upland Sandpiper *Bartramia longicauda*

Two known records, both in the Algarve: one in Ludo, Faro, in September 1999 and another one in Santa Luzia, Tavira, in September and October 2010.

135. Whimbrel *Numenius phaeopus*

An uncommon passage migrant and winter visitor, which is most frequently seen in coastal wetlands and rocky stretches of coastline close to the sea shore. Spring passage is mostly in April and May, whereas autumn passage occurs from August to October. Large numbers are sometimes seen on passage, especially in spring.

136. Eurasian Curlew *Numenius arquata*

An uncommon non-breeding visitor, which is really only met with in the large coastal wetlands; rather rare at small wetlands or away from the coast. Its main period of occurrence ranges from August to March, although there are a few records from other months.

137. Black-tailed Godwit *Limosa limosa*

A fairly common passage migrant and winter visitor, which occurs mainly in the large coastal wetlands and flooded areas; can also be found inland, albeit in smaller numbers. It is particularly abundant during migration periods; the pre-nuptial passage peaks in January and February, while the post-nuptial goes from July to October.

138. Bar-tailed Godwit *Limosa lapponica*

A passage migrant and winter visitor which is generally uncommon; it is most often found in the large coastal wetlands, where it can be locally common; sometimes it can also be found in small numbers in other places along the coast, particularly on migration. It is rare inland. A few non-breeders remain in the region throughout the breeding season.

139. Ruddy Turnstone *Arenaria interpres*

A common passage migrant and winter visitor which can be found along the entire coastline and, more rarely, inland. It is present mainly from August to May, but is occasionally recorded during the breeding season.

140. Red Knot *Calidris canutus*

A scarce but regular migrant and winter visitor, which occurs mainly along the coast, where it can be numerous during the pre-nuptial passage, especially during the first two weeks of May. Very rare inland.

141. Ruff *Calidris pugnax*

An uncommon passage migrant and rare winter visitor. It usually occurs in wetlands and is thus more frequent along the coastline, but sometimes it is seen inland. More common on passage, both pre-nuptial and post-nuptial, however a few birds overwinter.

142. Broad-billed Sandpiper *Calidris falcinellus*

Two recent records in the Algarve, both relating to single birds: one at Ria Formosa, in April 1997 and another one at Castro Marim in July 2012. There is also a reference to a bird seen in Tavira in 1973.

143. Curlew Sandpiper *Calidris ferruginea*

An uncommon passage migrant and very scarce winter visitor. It occurs at most coastal wetlands during the post-breeding migration, namely from August to October. Small numbers can also be seen during the pre-nuptial migration, especially in April and May, but there are records during other months as well. Not frequently seen away from the coast. A small population consisting of a few tens of birds may winter in the Algarve.

144. Temminck's Stint *Calidris temminckii*

A rare passage migrant which may occasionally overwinter. The species has been recorded at different times of the year, but seems to be more frequent between August and October.

145. Sanderling *Calidris alba*

A common passage migrant and winter visitor which can be seen along the coast, mainly on sandy or rocky beaches, but also in estuaries, saltpans and lagoons. Rather rare inland. It can be seen almost throughout the year and is more numerous from August to early May.

146. Dunlin *Calidris alpina*

A common non-breeding visitor, which occurs mostly at coastal wetlands and is occasionally seen inland.

147. Purple Sandpiper *Calidris maritima*

A rare winter visitor which can be found in very small numbers along the coastline, mostly in sectors with rocky beaches and also in breakwaters near harbours or river mouths.

148. Baird's Sandpiper *Calidris bairdii*

One at Ludo, Faro, in December 2004.

149. Little Stint *Calidris minuta*

A regular non-breeding visitor, usually in small numbers, although large flocks occur at times. Like most sandpipers, it occurs almost only along the coastline, mainly in estuaries and coastal lagoons. Rare in inland waters. More frequent on passage periods and in winter, it is very scarce during late spring and early summer.

150. White-rumped Sandpiper *Calidris fuscicollis*

Four records are known, all referring to single birds seen in the Algarve. One record is from the Ria de Alvor, the other three from the Sagres area. All sightings took place in October or November.

151. Buff-breasted Sandpiper *Calidris subruficollis*

A rare vagrant, which has been recorded on seven occasions, always in September or October. All records refer to single birds and were made at coastal locations in the Algarve.

152. Pectoral Sandpiper *Calidris melanotos*

About 14 records are known, the majority of them during the months of September and October, involving singletons or groups of two birds. Most records are from coastal wetlands, but there are a few sightings from inland locations.

153. Semipalmated Sandpiper *Calidris pusilla*

One trapped and ringed at Ria de Alvor in October 1989.

154. Wilson's Phalarope *Phalaropus tricolor*

A rare vagrant, which has been recorded on three occasions at several coastal wetlands in the Algarve.

155. Red-necked Phalarope *Phalaropus lobatus*

About eighteen records are known of this phalarope, almost all of them at coastal wetlands. Most records fall either in April, August or September.

156. Red Phalarope *Phalaropus fulicarius*

A rare passage migrant and winter visitor, which is probably frequent offshore, but which rarely approaches the coast, therefore there are very few records away from pelagic environment – the majority of these records were made after storms, when birds were seen in coastal wetlands. The period of occurrence ranges from August to March, however most records took place in autumn.

157. Terek Sandpiper *Xenus cinereus*

A rare vagrant, which has been recorded twice: one at Ria de Alvor in May 2000 and another one near Armação de Pera in September 2002.

158. Common Sandpiper *Actitis hypoleucos*

An uncommon species which can be found at all times of the year, usually in small numbers. It is not clear whether the breeding individuals are resident. In spring, this wader occurs throughout the region in low density. Outside the breeding season it is more frequently seen near the coast, mainly near wetlands, both on passage and in winter.

159. Spotted Sandpiper *Actitis macularius*

One in Vilamoura in September 2010.

160. Green Sandpiper *Tringa ochropus*

An uncommon passage migrant and winter visitor which can be seen mainly from January to March and again from late June until the end of the year. It occurs throughout the region.

161. Solitary Sandpiper *Tringa solitaria*

One at Ria de Alvor in June 1989.

162. Spotted Redshank *Tringa erythropus*

A regular but scarce non-breeding visitor, which occurs in coastal wetlands and, more rarely, inland. It is not infrequent on passage, both in spring and autumn; additionally, a few birds overwinter, mainly in the Algarve.

163. Common Greenshank *Tringa nebularia*

An uncommon passage migrant and winter visitor. It usually occurs near water bodies, mostly in coastal wetlands and sometimes inland. It can be seen mainly from August to April, but there are a few sightings outside this period.

164. Lesser Yellowlegs *Tringa flavipes*

A rare vagrant, with about 14 records, two thirds of them during the last quarter of the year. All sightings refer to single birds and almost all of them were made at coastal wetlands in the Algarve, with a single record from the Alentejo.

165. Marsh Sandpiper *Tringa stagnatilis*

A rare passage migrant, with about a dozen known records, all referring to single birds seen in the Algarve, most of them in the Castro Marim area. The months of August and September account for more than half of the existing records.

166. Wood Sandpiper *Tringa glareola*

A scarce but regular passage migrant, which occurs mainly between February and April and again between August and October and is occasionally recorded at other times of the year. Largely found in coastal wetlands, but sporadically recorded inland.

167. Common Redshank *Tringa totanus*

A common passage migrant and winter visitor, which occurs in all large and medium-sized coastal wetlands. Not often seen inland. It can be seen throughout the year, although it is scarce during the breeding season. Has bred occasionally in very small numbers at a few coastal wetlands in the eastern Algarve.

168. Jack Snipe *Lymnocryptes minimus*

An uncommon winter visitor, which is probably regular but is not frequently recorded, due to its shy habits. It is present mainly from September to March, with very few records during other months.

169. Long-billed Dowitcher *Limnodromus scolopaceus*

A rare vagrant, which has been recorded four times, of which three in the Algarve and one in the Alentejo. All records refer to singletons and took place in autumn.

170. Eurasian Woodcock *Scolopax rusticola*

An uncommon winter visitor, for which little is known about the distribution and population, due to its elusive habits. Probably occurs throughout the region, mostly from October to March.

171. Common Snipe *Gallinago gallinago*

A common and widespread non-breeding visitor, which is most numerous in flooded areas. It can be seen mainly from August to April.

172. Cream-coloured Courser *Cursorius cursor*

A rare vagrant from North Africa, which has been recorded on five occasions, four of them in the Algarve and the fifth one in the Alentejo plains. All records were made between March and August.

173. Collared Pratincole *Glareola pratincola*

An uncommon summer visitor, which breeds locally in the Alentejo and Algarve provinces. Arrives in late March and leaves in August.

174. Pomarine Skua *Stercorarius pomarinus*

An uncommon passage migrant, which is regular offshore; not infrequently, it is seen by land-based observers, usually in small numbers, but can be abundant when severe serial storms occur at sea. Pre-nuptial passage takes place in March and April, while post-nuptial passage ranges from August to November. Occasionally seen in winter.

175. Parasitic Jaeger *Stercorarius parasiticus*

An uncommon passage migrant, which is regularly seen on migration. Spring passage happens between March and May, whereas autumn passage takes place from August to October. This skua can also be found in very small numbers during the winter months.

176. Long-tailed Jaeger *Stercorarius longicaudus*

A scarce passage migrant which is only occasionally seen from land but which is probably regular offshore. Most known sightings were made from August to November, with a few records in spring. Cape St. Vincent is the place where this skua has been recorded more frequently.

177. Great Skua *Stercorarius skua*

An uncommon winter visitor which is regular at sea off the coast. It is often recorded from land, especially under bad weather conditions. It occurs mainly from September to March, with occasional sightings at other times of the year.

178. Common Murre *Uria aalge*

A very scarce winter visitor, which sometimes turns up along the coast, usually in small numbers.

179. Razorbill *Alca torda*

A fairly common winter visitor, which can regularly be seen from land, mainly from October to March. Sometimes it turns up in harbours or coastal wetlands.

180. Little Auk *Alle alle*

A rare vagrant to the region. Only three records are known, all from the west coast of the Algarve in autumn.

181. Atlantic Puffin *Fratercula arctica*

An uncommon passage migrant and winter visitor, which is probably regular offshore but is only occasionally seen from land. However, there are records of dead bodies found on beaches, usually after severe weather conditions. Its main period of occurrence extends from October to April.

182. Little Tern *Sternula albifrons*

An uncommon summer visitor and passage migrant. Breeds at the main coastal wetlands in the Algarve, especially in the eastern half. In the southern Alentejo it is very scarce, but might breed locally near some reservoirs. Turns up on migration at other locations. Its main period of occurrence ranges from April to September, but occasionally it is recorded in winter, especially in the Algarve.

183. Gull-billed Tern *Gelochelidon nilotica*

An uncommon summer migrant, which occurs mainly in the Alentejo, where it breeds near large or medium-sized reservoirs. In the Algarve it is scarce and turns up mainly during migration times. The main period of occurrence spans from April to September.

184. Caspian Tern *Hydroprogne caspia*

A scarce passage migrant and winter visitor that occurs in small numbers in wetlands along the Algarve south coast. Mostly recorded from September to April, with isolated records during other months. Only rarely seen in southern Alentejo.

185. Whiskered Tern *Chlidonias hybrida*

An uncommon summer visitor and passage migrant, which is highly irregular – it can be quite frequent in certain years and be almost totally absent in other years. Has bred in the Alentejo, mostly in marshes or reservoirs. When on migration, it can also be seen at coastal wetlands. Usually appears between April and September.

186. Black Tern *Chlidonias niger*

An uncommon passage migrant which turns up in highly variable numbers in different years. It occurs at coastal wetlands and sometimes inland as well. During post-nuptial passage it can also be found on the open sea. Spring passage usually takes place in April and May, autumn passage extends from August to October. Has bred in the Algarve.

187. White-winged Tern *Chlidonias leucopterus*

A rare passage migrant which has been recorded about 20 times. Sightings refer to single birds or groups of two and were made during the period ranging from April to October. Almost all records are from coastal locations in the Algarve, with two records from the Alentejo.

188. Sandwich Tern *Sterna sandvicensis*

A common passage migrant and uncommon winter visitor. It can be seen along the coast, and may be locally abundant on migration.

189. Royal Tern *Sterna maxima*

Only three records, all in the Algarve: the first at Ria de Alvor in October 1991; the second at the same place in April 1996; and the third one in the Castro Marim reserve in August 2006.

190. Lesser Crested Tern *Sterna bengalensis*

Five recent records, all during the period of post-breeding migration. Three records were made at Sagres, the other two at Salgados lagoon.

191. Forster's Tern *Sterna forsteri*

Two records are known: one at Castro Marim, in December 1993; another one at Fuseta, Olhão, in February 2003.

192. Common Tern *Sterna hirundo*

A fairly common passage migrant, which is recorded mostly near the coast and, occasionally, inland. Pre-nuptial passage occurs mostly in April and May, while post-nuptial passage ranges from August to October. However this tern is sometimes seen in other months, even in midwinter.

193. Roseate Tern *Sterna dougallii*

A very rare passage migrant, which has been recorded on three or four occasions along the Algarve south coast.

194. Arctic Tern *Sterna paradisaea*

An uncommon passage migrant which occurs regularly during migration periods along the coast, especially on the open sea.

195. Little Gull *Hydrocoloeus minutus*

A rare passage migrant and winter visitor, which can be found along the coast, both at coastal wetlands and on the open sea. Only seldom observed inland. Its main period of occurrence ranges from October to April, although there are some records on other months. Its numbers seem to vary a great deal between years.

196. Sabine's Gull *Xema sabini*

A passage migrant that is rare near the coast, but one that is probably frequent offshore, as there are several records from territorial waters and from the Exclusive Economic Zone. All records were made between April and November.

197. Black-legged Kittiwake *Rissa tridactyla*

An uncommon winter visitor which is probably numerous away from the coast, although only rarely seen close to land. It occurs largely from October to March, with a few records at other times of the year.

198. Slender-billed Gull *Larus genei*

Formerly considered a rarity, this gull is now regularly recorded in the eastern Algarve, especially around Tavira and in the Castro Marim reserve, near the mouth of the river Guadiana – there are many sightings from this area, in some cases involving tens of birds. In the western Algarve the species is very rare and only a few sporadic records are known from coastal wetlands.

199. Bonaparte's Gull *Larus philadelphia*

There are only two records, both involving single birds seen in the Algarve: the first near Faro in March 2011 and the second one near Vila Real de Santo António in February 2014.

200. Black-headed Gull *Larus ridibundus*

A common winter visitor and passage migrant, which occurs mainly from July to March, although a few birds stay around during the breeding season. It is generally more numerous near the coast than in the inland areas.

201. Laughing Gull *Larus atricilla*

Two birds at Sagres in December 2005.

202. Franklin's Gull *Larus pipixcan*

Two records: one at Salgados lagoon in November 2005 and the other one at Ria de Alvor in October 2015.

203. Audouin's Gull *Larus audouinii*

A fairly common passage migrant, which is mainly recorded in the eastern Algarve, where it occurs regularly on migration and where a few hundred birds overwinter. In the beginning of the 21st century this gull started to breed at Castro Marim and later at Ria Formosa, with more than one thousand pairs. In the western Algarve it is much less numerous, whereas in the Alentejo it is rarely recorded.

204. Mediterranean Gull *Larus melanocephalus*

A common passage migrant and winter visitor, which can be found along the entire coastline. The concentration of birds present at any given time fluctuates markedly. This gull can be seen throughout the year, however it is quite rare during spring time.

205. Mew Gull *Larus canus*

A scarce winter visitor which is recorded annually but almost always in small numbers. It is more frequent along the coast and is quite rare in inland areas. Mainly seen from November to March, with occasional records in other months.

206. Ring-billed Gull *Larus delawarensis*

A rare winter visitor which has been recorded on several occasions, with most records falling during winter months. Almost all records involved single birds or small flocks and were made at beaches, harbours and coastal wetlands. Very rarely recorded inland.

207. Kelp Gull *Larus dominicanus*

One at the Faro sewage works in August 2013.

208. Lesser Black-backed Gull *Larus fuscus*

An abundant passage migrant and winter visitor, which is seen mainly from July to March. It is more numerous along the coast, but can also be found inland, especially in the Alentejo. A few birds, mostly immature, remain in the region throughout the spring.

209. European Herring Gull *Larus argentatus*

A rare winter visitor, which has been recorded several times, mainly at beach locations, harbours or coastal wetlands. Most sightings refer to isolated birds or groups of two. Its period of occurrence ranges from September to March.

210. Caspian Gull *Larus cachinnans*

A first-summer bird was recorded at the Beja sanitary landfill, in April 2006. More recently, isolated birds were seen in the Algarve on two occasions.

211. Yellow-legged Gull *Larus michahellis*

An abundant resident which can be found along the entire coast. Breeds on islands, islets and on the rocky coast. In recent years it also started to nest in various coastal towns.

212. American Herring Gull *Larus smithsonianus*

One at Ludo, Faro, in December 1992.

213. Iceland Gull *Larus glaucoides*

A rare winter visitor, which has been recorded about 10 times, always near the coast. Several sightings took place at harbours. Most records took place between November and March and refer to single birds.

214. Glaucous Gull *Larus hyperboreus*

A rare winter visitor which is recorded almost every year in very small numbers. All records are from coastal areas, including harbours, and most took place from November to March, with a marked peak in January and February. There are isolated records from other times of the year.

215. Great Black-backed Gull *Larus marinus*

A rare winter visitor, which is recorded annually along the coast, almost always in very small numbers. Most sightings are from the period ranging from September to March, but there are occasional records outside this period.

216. Black-bellied Sandgrouse *Pterocles orientalis*

A rare resident with a discontinuous distribution, which occurs in the southern Alentejo, especially around Castro Verde and Mértola. The distribution area of this sandgrouse probably shrank during the 20th century.

217. Pin-tailed Sandgrouse *Pterocles alchata*

May have been regular in the past, but nowadays this sandgrouse is a rare vagrant to the region, with very few records from the Alentejo and only one from the Algarve, near the Spanish border.

218. Rock Dove *Columba livia*

A common and widespread resident. Domestic and feral populations can be found in most towns and villages, usually in close association with man. Small pockets of wild birds still survive in places along the rocky coast, but even here there are individual birds showing marks of the domestic type.

219. Stock Dove *Columba oenas*

An uncommon winter visitor, which occurs on autumn passage along the coast and during winter in the Alentejo, usually in small numbers. There are scattered records during the breeding season, but it is not clear whether the species nests in the region.

220. Common Wood Pigeon *Columba palumbus*

A locally common resident and winter visitor. As a breeding bird it is found over most of the region, although it is scarce in the western part of the Alentejo and in coastal areas of the Algarve. In the winter, large flocks occur in the Alentejo, sometimes with thousands of birds involved. Migrating parties also appear near the coastline at times.

221. Eurasian Collared Dove *Streptopelia decaocto*

Has colonized the country during the last quarter of the 20th century and is nowadays a widespread and common bird throughout the region.

222. European Turtle Dove *Streptopelia turtur*

This summer visitor occurs over most of the region but its abundance varies markedly: it is quite common in the eastern Algarve and rather uncommon elsewhere. It occurs regularly on migration, particularly along the coast. The national population of this dove has been declining for several decades.

223. Rose-ringed Parakeet *Psittacula krameri*

An uncommon and localised resident. This parakeet is native to Asia and Africa but was introduced to Portugal, probably during the 1970s. A small wild population became established in Lisbon and in the surrounding areas. In the region covered by this book it is a rare bird, scattered records are known from several places but there is no evidence of regular breeding.

224. Great Spotted Cuckoo *Clamator glandarius*

An uncommon summer visitor, which breeds mostly in the eastern half of the Alentejo and is rather scarce elsewhere. It is an early migrant that arrives in late January and leaves in July, although there are a few records outside this period. This species is a parasite and lays its eggs in the nests of corvids, showing a preference for those of the Common Magpie.

225. Common Cuckoo *Cuculus canorus*

A common summer visitor, which can be heard from late February onwards. After mid June, males become silent and this cuckoo is then difficult to locate, although it is known to occur until September. Like the preceding species, it is a parasite – its victims are mainly the smaller passerines.

226. Barn Owl *Tyto alba*

A fairly common and widespread resident.

227. Eurasian Scops Owl *Otus scops*

This is an uncommon summer visitor, which occurs mostly between March and October. It has a widespread distribution, especially in the eastern half of the region, but usually occurs in low density. It is regularly recorded on passage away from breeding areas, particularly along the coast of Algarve. A few winter records are known.

228. Eurasian Eagle-Owl *Bubo bubo*

An uncommon resident, which occurs mostly in remote inland areas, but locally also closer to the coast. It seems to be more numerous along the valley of the Guadiana, as well as along those of its tributaries.

229. Little Owl *Athene noctua*

A common and widespread resident.

230. Tawny Owl *Strix aluco*

An uncommon resident which occurs throughout the region in low density. It is more frequent in the western part of the Alentejo and in certain parts of inner Algarve.

231. Long-eared Owl *Asio otus*

A rare resident. Its distribution area is poorly known, due to its shy habits. Probably occurs over most of the region, usually at low density. Outside the breeding season it is sometimes found close to the coast, in places where breeding is not known.

232. Short-eared Owl *Asio flammeus*

A rare winter visitor, which arrives in late September and stays until March or April. It seems to be more frequent close to the coast, especially near wetlands. There are very few records inland, although the species is known to occur at times in cereal fields in the eastern part of the Alentejo.

233. European Nightjar *Caprimulgus europaeus*

An uncommon passage migrant. Spring passage takes place in April and May, while autumn passage happens in September and October.

234. Red-necked Nightjar *Caprimulgus ruficollis*

A fairly common summer visitor, which breeds over most of the region. It occurs from April to September.

235. Chimney Swift *Chaetura pelagica*

One at Salgados lagoon and five at Sagres, all in October 1999. Another one at Sagres in September 2013.

236. Common Swift *Apus apus*

A common summer visitor, which is usually present from March to October, with a few records during the wintering period. Large flocks pass through the area during migration periods.

237. Pallid Swift *Apus pallidus*

A common summer visitor, this swift is widespread as a breeding species, but its distribution area is largely discontinuous. It seems to be more frequent along the south coast than elsewhere. It occurs mainly between March and September and is rarely recorded outside this period.

238. Alpine Swift *Apus melba*

An uncommon and localised summer visitor which breeds on cliffs, mainly along the coast. It is also a scarce passage migrant. Its main period of occurrence ranges from March to October.

239. White-rumped Swift *Apus caffer*

A rare summer visitor, which arrives in May and leaves in September, although there are a few records outside the main period of occurrence. Breeding has been confirmed in both the eastern Alentejo and the Algarve.

240. Little Swift *Apus affinis*

Nine records are known, of which six in the Algarve and three in the Alentejo. Two thirds of the sightings were made during May or June, whereas the remaining ones took place between March and October.

241. Common Kingfisher *Alcedo atthis*

A resident and dispersive species which occurs throughout the region. Generally uncommon and mostly seen isolated or in pairs. It is frequent in the largest wetlands, especially outside the breeding season.

242. European Bee-eater *Merops apiaster*

A common summer visitor, which occurs throughout the region. Usually arrives in late March and leaves in mid September.

243. Blue-cheeked Bee-eater *Merops persicus*

One at Piçarras, Castro Verde, in April 2014.

244. European Roller *Coracias garrulus*

A scarce summer visitor, which occurs almost exclusively in the open plains of the inner Alentejo, especially around Castro Verde. Birds on passage can turn up elsewhere, namely near the coastline. It is usually found between April and mid September.

245. Hoopoe *Upupa epops*

A partial migrant which occurs throughout the region and is generally a common bird. It can be seen year round.

246. Eurasian Wryneck *Jynx torquilla*

An uncommon summer breeder and passage migrant, the Wryneck has a very patchy distribution covering several areas of the region. It occurs mostly between April and October, but occasionally it is recorded during the winter months.

247. European Green Woodpecker *Picus viridis*

This resident woodpecker can be found over most of the region, although it seems to be largely absent in certain parts of the Alentejo. Birds belong to the Iberian race *sharpei*, which some authorities accept as a full species.

248. Great Spotted Woodpecker *Dendrocopos major*

A fairly common and widespread resident which is generally more frequent in the western half.

249. Lesser Spotted Woodpecker *Dendrocopos minor*

An uncommon resident with a wide but discontinuous range. It is more frequent in the Algarve and in the western half of southern Alentejo.

250. Calandra Lark *Melanocorypha calandra*

An uncommon resident which occurs mainly in the open plains of central Alentejo, especially around Beja and Castro Verde. Very rare in the Algarve.

251. Greater Short-toed Lark *Calandrella brachydactyla*

An uncommon summer visitor which in the Algarve occurs chiefly near the coast, while in the Alentejo it is more often found in the open plains. It can be seen mainly from late March to late September.

252. Lesser Short-toed Lark *Calandrella rufescens*

A rare resident which occurs only in the Castro Marim reserve, where there is a small breeding population of a few tens of pairs. Very rarely reported from other places in the Algarve.

253. Crested Lark *Galerida cristata*

A common and widespread resident, although its distribution area has some gaps in southeastern Alentejo.

254. Thekla Lark *Galerida theklae*

A common resident, which occurs over much of Algarve and Alentejo. Generally it is more frequent in the eastern half of the region.

255. Woodlark *Lullula arborea*

A fairly common and widespread resident.

256. Eurasian Skylark *Alauda arvensis*

A common winter visitor. From October to March, wintering birds can be found throughout the region and are numerous in all types of open ground. A very small resident population is known from the Sagres area, where it probably breeds.

257. Sand Martin *Riparia riparia*

An uncommon summer visitor and passage migrant, which may breed locally in small numbers along the Alentejo coast. Usually occurs from February to September.

258. Eurasian Crag Martin *Ptyonoprogne rupestris*

Resident or partially migratory, this hirundine is widespread but generally uncommon. It is present in the region throughout the year. Breeds mainly inland, but during the cold season it is more frequently recorded near the coastline, away from known breeding areas.

259. Barn Swallow *Hirundo rustica*

An abundant and widespread summer visitor. It arrives from January onwards and leaves for Africa between August and October. Occasionally it is recorded during the last two months of the year.

260. Common House Martin *Delichon urbicum*

A common summer visitor which occurs mainly from mid-January to October, with a few isolated records during the remaining months.

261. Red-rumped Swallow *Cecropis daurica*

A fairly common summer visitor. It is more numerous in the eastern parts of Alentejo and Algarve than elsewhere. It usually arrives in late February and leaves until early November.

262. Richard's Pipit *Anthus richardi*

A rare winter visitor which has been recorded in most years, albeit in very small numbers. Several tens of records are known of isolated birds or small parties, from various coastal locations. This pipit occurs mainly between October and April, with scattered records outside this period.

263. Blyth's Pipit *Anthus godlewskii*

One at Malhão, Odemira, in March 2003.

264. Tawny Pipit *Anthus campestris*

An uncommon summer visitor and passage migrant, which also breeds locally in certain open areas, especially along the west coast and in central Alentejo. It is present mainly from April to October, but occasionally it has been recorded at other times.

265. Olive-backed Pipit *Anthus hodgsoni*

A very rare vagrant which was first recorded at Ria de Alvor in November 1994; more recently there were some records of birds on autumn migration near Cape St. Vincent in 2014.

266. Tree Pipit *Anthus trivialis*

A fairly common passage migrant, which is more numerous during post-nuptial migration than on the pre-nuptial one. Its normal period of occurrence ranges from March to Abril and from August to early November.

267. Meadow Pipit *Anthus pratensis*

An abundant non-breeding visitor which occurs from late September to early April.

268. Red-throated Pipit *Anthus cervinus*

A rare vagrant which has been recorded about 15 times, both in the Algarve and in the Alentejo. All sightings were of single birds or groups of two. About one third of the records were made in April, the remaining ones were between September and February.

269. Water Pipit *Anthus spinoletta*

An uncommon winter visitor, which turns up during the cold season, chiefly from October to March, at most coastal wetlands, where it can be locally common. Much less frequent inland, where it occurs near water bodies.

270. Eurasian Rock Pipit *Anthus petrosus*

A rare but seemingly regular winter visitor, for which there are several records of single birds or small parties. All records were made along the coastline, Sagres harbour being the place with the largest number of sightings. The period of occurrence ranges from late October to February.

271. Yellow Wagtail *Motacilla flava*

A summer visitor which occurs mostly at coastal wetlands. It is generally uncommon, but it can be locally numerous. Can turn up on passage at other places away from breeding areas and on these occasions other subspecies are frequently recorded. It can usually be seen from February until October.

272. Citrine Wagtail *Motacilla citreola*

One at the Arade estuary, Portimão, in March 1997.

273. Grey Wagtail *Motacilla cinerea*

An uncommon resident. As a breeding bird, it occurs in low density, mainly in the inner Algarve, but is largely absent from most of the southern Alentejo. During autumn and winter it becomes more frequent in places where it does not breed, including in coastal areas, where it can usually be seen from October to March.

274. White Wagtail *Motacilla alba*

An uncommon resident which breeds sparsely in the eastern half of the Alentejo and is very infrequent elsewhere. However, during autumn and winter it is common throughout the region.

275. White-throated Dipper *Cinclus cinclus*

One at Ribeira de Asseca, Tavira, in May 1997.

276. Winter Wren *Troglodytes troglodytes*

A common resident. It is more numerous in the western half, its abundance dropping sharply as one moves eastwards. The basin of the river Guadiana, near the border with Spain, holds the lowest densities.

277. Dunnock *Prunella modularis*

An uncommon winter visitor, which occurs from October to March.

278. Alpine Accentor *Prunella collaris*

A rare but regular winter visitor, which is present mainly from October to March. It has a localised distribution and occurs only at specific locations, usually near cliffs. The rocky bluffs at Cape St. Vincent is one place where it seems to be more frequent, but even there it is usually seen in small numbers only.

279. Rufous-tailed Scrub Robin *Cercotrichas galactotes*

A scarce summer visitor which breeds mainly in the basin of the Guadiana river, corresponding broadly to the eastern parts of the Alentejo and Algarve provinces. Birds on passage are sporadically recorded near the coast. Its main period of occurrence extends from May to August, with very few records outside this period.

280. European Robin *Erithacus rubecula*

An abundant winter visitor which occurs throughout the area from October to March. Breeds in far smaller numbers in the Serras of Monchique and Caldeirão and also along the southwest coast, where it favours valleys with trees or scrub.

281. Common Nightingale *Luscinia megarhynchos*

A common summer visitor and passage migrant, which occurs from late March until September, sometimes later.

282. Bluethroat *Luscinia svecica*

An uncommon passage migrant and winter visitor, which occurs mainly from September to March. Largely coastal in its distribution, mainly around wetlands (with salt marsh or reed beds), it is quite rare inland.

283. Red-flanked Bluetail *Tarsiger cyanurus*

One trapped and killed in Boliqueime, Loulé, in January 2012.

284. Black Redstart *Phoenicurus ochruros*

A fairly common resident and winter visitor. Rather localised as a breeding bird, it occurs mainly on coastal cliffs, with very few records inland. Between October and March it is widespread and can frequently be found elsewhere, away from breeding areas.

285. Common Redstart *Phoenicurus phoenicurus*

An uncommon summer visitor and passage migrant. It has a discontinuous distribution and seems to be more frequent in the Algarve hills than elsewhere. On migration it often turns up in places where it does not breed, particularly along the coast. It usually occurs from March to October.

286. Moussier's Redstart *Phoenicurus moussieri*

A male at Sagres, Vila do Bispo, between November 2006 and January 2007.

287. Whinchat *Saxicola rubetra*

A fairly common passage migrant, which is more frequent during the post-nuptial passage than on the pre-nuptial. The main period of occurrence in autumn extends from September to early November, while spring passage peaks in April.

288. Siberian Stonechat *Saxicola maurus*

One at Ponta da Atalaia, Aljezur, in October 1997.

289. European Stonechat *Saxicola rubicola*

A common resident, which occurs throughout the region. It is particularly abundant in the Alentejo. In certain parts of the Algarve it is apparently a non-breeding visitor.

290. Northern Wheatear *Oenanthe oenanthe*

An abundant passage migrant during the post-nuptial passage, which can extend well into November. Small numbers occur on spring migration.

291. Black-eared Wheatear *Oenanthe hispanica*

An uncommon summer visitor, which occurs mainly in the eastern half of the region. Its distribution area is somewhat discontinuous. It is more frequent in the Castro Verde, Mértola and Alcoutim areas. The period of occurrence extends from March to September.

292. White-crowned Wheatear *Oenanthe leucopyga*

One at Ria de Alvor in March 2001.

293. Black Wheatear *Oenanthe leucura*

Formerly bred at Noudar castle, near Barrancos, but this is no longer the case and this wheatear is now extirpated in the region.

294. Common Rock Thrush *Monticola saxatilis*

A rare passage migrant, which has occasionally been recorded in coastal lowlands and also at Serra de Monchique, where it seems to be almost annual.

295. Blue Rock Thrush *Monticola solitarius*

An uncommon resident with a rather patchy distribution. In the Algarve it is widespread and occurs over most of the province, whereas in the Alentejo it can be seen along the rocky coast and also in the eastern half, mainly along the valley of the river Guadiana and those of its tributaries.

296. Ring Ouzel *Turdus torquatus*

A very scarce non-breeding visitor which occurs mostly from October to April. Most records are from the Algarve, both near the coast and inland.

297. Common Blackbird *Turdus merula*

A very numerous resident which is generally abundant, except in more open areas of the Alentejo, where it is uncommon.

298. Fieldfare *Turdus pilaris*

A scarce winter visitor which occurs from October to March. The number of birds wintering in the region fluctuates, but in most years the Fieldfare can be considered a rare bird.

299. Song Thrush *Turdus philomelos*

An abundant winter visitor that can be seen between October and April.

300. Redwing *Turdus iliacus*

A winter visitor, its abundance can vary markedly from year to year – it can be very common in certain years and quite scarce in other years. It occurs throughout the region and can be seen mainly from mid October to March, often forming mixed parties with other species of thrush.

301. Mistle Thrush *Turdus viscivorus*

An uncommon resident which occurs over most of the region, usually in low density.

302. Cetti's Warbler *Cettia cetti*

A common and widespread resident. Its abundance varies markedly between regions: this warbler is generally more frequent in coastal areas than inland.

303. Zitting Cisticola *Cisticola juncidis*

A very common and widespread resident.

304. Common Grasshopper Warbler *Locustella naevia*

An uncommon passage migrant, which is recorded mainly on post-nuptial passage, from August to October. Rare during the pre-nuptial migration, with a few records between late March and early May.

305. Savi's Warbler *Locustella luscinioides*

A rare and localised summer visitor. It can only be found at certain coastal wetlands with reed beds or other type of emergent vegetation, namely along the Algarve south coast. Only rarely recorded on migration away from breeding areas.

306. Booted Warbler *Iduna caligata*

One near Sagres in October 2015.

307. Western Olivaceous Warbler *Iduna opaca*

A very rare summer visitor which may not occur regularly. Its distribution area is poorly known. Most records are from the basin of the river Guadiana, with scattered records from other locations. The existing records range from late April until October.

308. Icterine Warbler *Hippolais icterina*

A very rare vagrant, which has been recorded in the Algarve on three occasions only. There are two autumn records, both at Ria de Alvor in autumn 1997, and one spring record, involving a bird seen near Faro in May 2015.

309. Melodious Warbler *Hippolais polyglotta*

A common summer migrant which breeds throughout the region and occurs chiefly from mid April to mid September.

310. Moustached Warbler *Acrocephalus melanopogon*

Probably a rare vagrant, but its status remains unclear. Three recent records are known from the Algarve. Two of them took place in October and one in March.

311. Aquatic Warbler *Acrocephalus paludicola*

A rare passage migrant which is hard to see due to its elusive habits. It has only been recorded on post-nuptial passage. Most records were made at coastal wetlands and refer mainly to birds caught in mist nets during ringing sessions. Its period of occurrence extends from August to October.

312. Sedge Warbler *Acrocephalus schoenobaenus*

An uncommon passage migrant which can be seen during both the pre-nuptial passage, from mid-February to April, and the post-nuptial one, from mid-July to October. It has been recorded both in the Algarve and in the Alentejo and seems to be more common in coastal wetlands, but its shy habits make detection difficult.

313. Paddyfield Warbler *Acrocephalus agricola*

One at Ria de Alvor in November 1993 and another one at Vilamoura in October 2014.

314. Eurasian Reed Warbler *Acrocephalus scirpaceus*

Uncommon as a summer visitor and common on passage. It occurs mainly in the Algarve, but sometimes it is also found at certain places in the Alentejo. It is usually seen between mid March and early November.

315. Great Reed Warbler *Acrocephalus arundinaceus*

An uncommon summer visitor. It occurs from late March to early September, with odd records outside this period.

316. Dartford Warbler *Sylvia undata*

A locally common resident which occurs over much of the region, although it is scarce in much of the Alentejo province. Most often found in scrub-covered areas. During the cold season it is regularly recorded in areas where it does not breed, namely in coastal lowlands.

317. Spectacled Warbler *Sylvia conspicillata*

This is an uncommon breeding migrant, which has a patchy distribution. It occurs mostly over the eastern half of the Alentejo, but also breeds locally near the coast in the Algarve. Tends to favour dry areas with low scrub. Its main period of occurrence ranges from March to October.

318. Subalpine Warbler *Sylvia cantillans*

An uncommon summer visitor which occurs from March to October. The main areas in which to find this species lie in the eastern half, however it can also be found at certain places further west. When on passage it is regularly recorded near the coast.

319. Sardinian Warbler *Sylvia melanocephala*

An abundant and widespread resident.

320. Western Orphean Warbler *Sylvia hortensis*

An uncommon summer visitor, which breeds chiefly in the eastern Alentejo. In the Algarve it is very scarce and occurs mainly on passage, although it breeds locally. It is usually present between April and August.

321. Lesser Whitethroat *Sylvia curruca*

Two records are known from the last 20 years, both of them at Cape St. Vincent: the first was made in October 1994 and the other one in September 2011.

322. Common Whitethroat *Sylvia communis*

A common passage migrant which can be found throughout the region, more often on post-nuptial passage than on the pre-nuptial one. A very small breeding population is known from the peak of Serra de Monchique.

323. Garden Warbler *Sylvia borin*

A common passage migrant, which occurs throughout the area, mainly between August and October, sometimes as late as November. On pre-nuptial passage it is scarce, with most records in April and May.

324. Eurasian Blackcap *Sylvia atricapilla*

A fairly common resident and an abundant winter visitor. During the breeding season, it is common in some areas, but it is largely absent from much of the inner Alentejo. In winter it is very numerous, even in places where it does not breed.

325. Pallas's Leaf Warbler *Phylloscopus proregulus*

There are two records of this species: the first at Barranco do Velho, Loulé, in December 1990 and the other one at Barão de São João, Lagos, in December 2002.

326. Yellow-browed Warbler *Phylloscopus inornatus*

A rare passage migrant, which has been sporadically recorded during post-breeding migration. About 45 records are known, almost all of them in October and November. More records were made in the Algarve. There are two spring records: a bird was seen in April 2001, near Albufeira and another one at Vila Nova de Milfontes in April 2011.

327. Hume's Leaf Warbler *Phylloscopus humei*

One near Sagres in October 2015 was the first record for Portugal.

328. Dusky Warbler *Phylloscopus fuscatus*

A very rare vagrant, which has been recorded on four occasions, all of them in late October or during November.

329. Western Bonelli's Warbler *Phylloscopus bonelli*

An uncommon passage migrant, which might breed locally. Can be seen mainly between April and September, with occasional records outside this period.

330. Wood Warbler *Phylloscopus sibilatrix*

A rare vagrant or perhaps a regular passage migrant in very small numbers. About a dozen records are known from the Algarve, all during the months of April, May and September.

331. Common Chiffchaff *Phylloscopus collybita*

An abundant winter visitor, which is most numerous in coastal lowlands. It occurs in the region mainly from October to March.

332. Iberian Chiffchaff *Phylloscopus ibericus*

A fairly common summer visitor, which occurs over most of the Algarve and in the western half of the southern Alentejo. It can be seen mainly between late February and September.

333. Willow Warbler *Phylloscopus trochilus*

A very common passage migrant which is more numerous during post-nuptial passage (from late July to early November) than on the pre-nuptial one (March to mid-May).

334. Goldcrest *Regulus regulus*

A very scarce winter visitor, which occurs mainly between November and March.

335. Common Firecrest *Regulus ignicapilla*

A scarce resident and an uncommon winter visitor. As a breeding bird it occurs in very small numbers in the Algarve hills, namely Serra de Monchique and Serra do Caldeirão. During the winter months it is widespread.

336. Spotted Flycatcher *Muscicapa striata*

A very scarce summer visitor, which occurs in low densities, mostly in the hills of inland Algarve. It is also a passage migrant, which is sometimes common on post-nuptial passage, from August to early November, and uncommon on pre-nuptial passage, which takes place in April and May.

337. Red-breasted Flycatcher *Ficedula parva*

A vagrant species or possibly a very rare passage migrant, which has been sporadically recorded on autumn migration. About nine records are known, all in the Algarve and mostly in October or November, but there is one case of a bird that overwintered.

338. European Pied Flycatcher *Ficedula hypoleuca*

An abundant passage migrant during post-nuptial migration; it can be seen from late July until early November and is especially numerous during the month of September. Rather scarce on pre-nuptial migration, it is sometimes recorded in early spring, when winds blow from the east.

339. Long-tailed Tit *Aegithalos caudatus*

A fairly common and widespread resident. Birds of southern Portugal belong to the race *A. c. irbii*, which has a grey back.

340. Eurasian Blue Tit *Cyanistes caeruleus*

A common resident which occurs throughout the region. It is particularly abundant in the western part of the Alentejo.

341. Great Tit *Parus major*

An abundant and widespread resident.

342. European Crested Tit *Lophophanes cristatus*

An uncommon resident which occurs over most of the region. It is a bird of woodland which shows a marked preference for conifers. It is very scarce over much of the inner Alentejo, due to the lack of suitable habitat.

343. Eurasian Nuthatch *Sitta europaea*

A resident species which occurs throughout the area. It is more numerous in the western half and it is very scarce in the lower basin of the river Guadiana, in the southeast.

344. Wallcreeper *Tichodroma muraria*

One in Loulé in November 2008.

345. Short-toed Treecreeper *Certhia brachydactyla*

A widespread resident which is fairly common throughout the region, except in southeastern Alentejo and northeastern Algarve, where it is scarce.

346. Eurasian Penduline Tit *Remiz pendulinus*

A regular winter visitor in small numbers, which can be seen mainly between October and March. It is more frequent is coastal areas than inland. Breeding was confirmed near Mértola in 2003.

347. Eurasian Golden Oriole *Oriolus oriolus*

An uncommon but widespread summer visitor which occurs over most of the region. Its abundance is highly variable and the species is generally scarce in the western half and more common in the east. The areas of greatest abundance lie in the area of lower Guadiana, namely around Alcoutim and Mértola. It occurs mainly between mid-April and mid-September.

348. Red-backed Shrike *Lanius collurio*

One at Sagres in October 1994.

349. Southern Grey Shrike *Lanius meridionalis*

An uncommon but widespread resident, possibly also a winter visitor. It is clearly more numerous in the open plains of central Alentejo than elsewhere.

350. Woodchat Shrike *Lanius senator*

A common summer visitor which arrives in March and leaves in September. It occurs throughout the region and it is generally more abundant in the Alentejo, especially in the areas lying close to the Spanish border. Seems to have declined, at least in some parts of its range.

351. Eurasian Jay *Garrulus glandarius*

A common and widespread resident.

352. Azure-winged Magpie *Cyanopica cyanus*

A very common resident which is more abundant in the east, along the basin of the river Guadiana and also along the Algarve south coast.

353. Common Magpie *Pica pica*

A common resident in the eastern Alentejo. Elsewhere it is scarce, but can be found in small numbers along the coast of the Algarve.

354. Red-billed Chough *Pyrrhocorax pyrrhocorax*

A scarce and local resident, which occurs mainly around Sagres and Cape St. Vincent. Very rarely seen elsewhere.

355. Western Jackdaw *Corvus monedula*

A scarce resident with a highly discontinuous distribution; it occurs mainly along the rocky coast, west of Lagoa, and also in the eastern Alentejo, along the Guadiana basin. Its population has dropped markedly at several coastal locations.

356. Rook *Corvus frugilegus*

A very rare vagrant from other European countries. Only one record is known from the last 50 years: one at Odelouca, Silves, in December 1987.

357. Carrion Crow *Corvus corone*

In the southern Alentejo this bird is a common resident. In the Algarve it is very scarce and it occurs only in the northwestern tip, around Aljezur.

358. Northern Raven *Corvus corax*

An uncommon resident, which occurs mostly inland, locally also along the coast.

359. Spotless Starling *Sturnus unicolor*

A common and widespread resident which is especially abundant in the Alentejo.

360. Common Starling *Sturnus vulgaris*

A common winter visitor which can be seen mainly between October and February. It probably occurs throughout the region, however its distribution area and its abundance are masked, due to confusion with the Spotless Starling, with which it often associates.

361. Rosy Starling *Pastor roseus*

About ten records are known, referring either to single birds or to groups of two. Almost all sightings refer to young birds, mostly seen during the months of September, October and November. The place with the largest number of sightings is Cape St. Vincent (more than half of all records), the remaining ones come from various other locations in the Algarve or in the Alentejo, most of them near the coast.

362. House Sparrow *Passer domesticus*

A very common resident, which occurs throughout the region.

363. Spanish Sparrow *Passer hispaniolensis*

Breeds over much of the southern Alentejo and also in the northeastern Algarve, namely around Alcoutim. Its colonies can congregate many hundreds of pairs. During winter many birds move to coastal wetlands, away from breeding grounds.

364. Eurasian Tree Sparrow *Passer montanus*

This is an uncommon but widespread resident. Its distribution is quite patchy and the species is absent from much of the eastern Alentejo.

365. Rock Sparrow *Petronia petronia*

An uncommon resident which occurs mostly in the Alentejo, where it can be locally numerous, especially in the eastern tip, around Barrancos. In the Algarve it is a scarce bird, but there are many autumn records from the Cape St. Vincent area and several winter records from other locations.

366. White-winged Snowfinch *Montifringilla nivalis*

A very rare vagrant, which has been recorded in the Algarve on two occasions only: two birds were seen at Cape St. Vincent in December 1998 and January 1999, and another one was found at ribeira de Aljezur in January 2016.

367. Black-headed Weaver *Ploceus melanocephalus*

A very scarce and localised resident. This weaver is native to the Afrotropics and it was introduced in the country during the 1990s. It can nowadays be seen in the central Algarve, where it occurs at coastal wetlands, usually with reedbeds or other type of emergent vegetation.

368. Yellow-crowned Bishop *Euplectes afer*

An uncommon and localised resident. This bird, which is native to Africa, was probably introduced during the second half of the 1980s. It has been recorded on several occasions at Quinta do Lago and Lagoa dos Patos, with a few records from other locations.

369. Common Waxbill *Estrilda astrild*

A common resident, which is native to sub-Saharan Africa. It was introduced in Portugal in the 1960s. Currently it can be found over most of the Algarve and also in the western part of the southern Alentejo. It is, however, rather scarce in the eastern half of the latter province.

370. Red Avadavat *Amandava amandava*

A scarce non-native resident, which originates from Asia and was introduced in the country. It has a very discontinuous distribution. Its presence has been recorded at several locations, both in the Alentejo and in the Algarve, but its current status is not very clear.

371. Common Chaffinch *Fringilla coelebs*

A very common resident and winter visitor. As a breeding species it is more numerous in the western half of the region and is scarcer in the east. During the winter it can also be found in the areas where it is rare or absent during the breeding season.

372. Brambling *Fringilla montifringilla*

A rare winter visitor which is usually recorded between October and March, however its numbers fluctuate markedly between years.

373. European Serin *Serinus serinus*

A common resident in the Algarve and in the western part of the Alentejo, which is however scarce in the open treeless plains around Castro Verde and Mértola.

374. European Greenfinch *Carduelis chloris*

A common resident which occurs throughout the region. It is more frequent in the Algarve.

375. European Goldfinch *Carduelis carduelis*

An abundant and widespread resident.

376. European Siskin *Carduelis spinus*

This is a winter visitor which can be seen in the region between October and March. Its abundance shows marked fluctuations between years and the Siskin is quite common in some years and rather scarce in others.

377. Common Linnet *Carduelis cannabina*

A widespread resident which is generally common.

378. Common Redpoll *Carduelis flammea*

A very rare vagrant from Central and Northern Europe, which has been recorded on one occasion only: a bird was seen near Cape St. Vincent in October 2013.

379. Red Crossbill *Loxia curvirostra*

A rare passage and wintering species. In most years it is very scarce and there are few records or none at all; however, in irruption years, numbers surge and Crossbills are then recorded in good numbers – this was the case in 1990 and 1993.

380. Common Rosefinch *Carpodacus erythrinus*

A very rare vagrant, which has only been recorded on autumn passage: six records are known, all between mid September and early November.

381. Eurasian Bullfinch *Pyrrhula pyrrhula*

A scarce winter visitor. which can be seen from mid October to late March, mostly at inland locations.

382. Hawfinch *Coccothraustes coccothraustes*

A widespread but scarce resident with a patchy distribution. Nowhere common. It seems to be slightly more frequent in the Guadiana basin.

383. Common Yellowthroat *Geothlypis trichas*

A first winter male was trapped and ringed at Vilamoura in October 2010.

384. Snow Bunting *Plectrophenax nivalis*

A rare winter visitor that has been recorded in very small numbers at several locations in the Algarve, mainly between November and February. Most records are from coastal sites, such as dunes, capes and river mouths.

385. Yellowhammer *Emberiza citrinella*

A rare vagrant to the region. The only recent record refers to a male recorded at Cape St. Vincent in November 2011.

386. Cirl Bunting *Emberiza cirlus*

An uncommon resident, which occurs mainly in the western part of the region, especially along the west coast. It becomes increasingly uncommon as one moves east and is very scarce in the basin of the river Guadiana and over much of the eastern Algarve.

387. Rock Bunting *Emberiza cia*

This bunting is resident but its distribution is discontinuous. It is a scarce bird, which occurs mainly in the hills of the inner Algarve, but small numbers can also be found in the eastern Alentejo, mainly along the Guadiana basin and in certain hills in the western part of this region.

388. Ortolan Bunting *Emberiza hortulana*

An uncommon passage migrant, which is regularly recorded in autumn in coastal lowlands, mainly in September and October. Rarely seen during the pre-nuptial passage.

389. Rustic Bunting *Emberiza rustica*

Only two records are known, both referring to single birds in the Algarve: the first was at the Ria de Alvor in November 1990 and the other one was on the rice fields of Nossa Senhora do Rosário, Lagoa, in December 2008.

390. Little Bunting *Emberiza pusilla*

A very rare vagrant, which has been recorded four times. All records refer to single birds and were made at different places in the Algarve. Three of them took place in November and the other one in March.

391. Common Reed Bunting *Emberiza schoeniclus*

An uncommon wintering species, which occurs mostly in coastal lowlands, although it is also found at inland sites. Tends to favour wet areas, such as reed beds, marshes and agricultural fields with ditches covered by emergent vegetation.

392. Corn Bunting *Emberiza calandra*

An abundant resident. It is widespread in the region and is especially numerous in the plains of the Alentejo.

Appendix: Species of uncertain origin

This section comprises 9 species that have been recorded, for whose wild provenance some doubts remain or cannot now be ascertained. Although it is possible that they are genuine vagrants that arrived in the country naturally, the possibility of their being escapes from captivity cannot be excluded.

393. Mute Swan *Cygnus olor*

Two records exist, both referring to single birds. The first was at Vilamoura in July 2007 and the other one at Salgados lagoon in March 2008.

394. Bar-headed Goose *Anser indicus*

Two were at the Tavira salt pans in February 2000.

395. Canada Goose *Branta canadensis*

One bird stayed at Salgados lagoon from September 2002 until March 2003.

396. Great White Pelican *Pelecanus onocrotalus*

One at Lagoa dos Patos, Alvito, in October 2007.

397. Marabou Stork *Leptoptilos crumenifer*

One was seen at Morgado do Reguengo, Portimão, in August 2004.

398. Lesser Flamingo *Phoenicopterus minor*

Five records are known, all from the Algarve and all involving one or two birds, usually among flocks of Greater

Flamingos. Three records were made in February or March, the other two are from summer months.

399. White-backed Vulture *Gyps africanus*

One was photographed at Cape St. Vincent in October 2006.

400. Gyrfalcon *Falco rusticolus*

One at Malhão, Odemira, and also at Odeceixe, Aljezur, in March 1991.

401. Laughing Dove *Streptopelia senegalensis*

One was recorded at Mexilhoeira Grande, Portimão, in April 2008.

Bibliography

Aves de Portugal – o portal dos observadores de aves. Available online at: http://www.avesdeportugal.info. Viewed 27 February 2016.

BirdLife - www.birdlife.org – official site of BirdLife International

British Ornithologists' Union. Species categories. Available online at: http://www.bou.org.uk/british-list/species-categories/ - site oficial da British Ornithologists' Union. Viewed 27 February 2016.

Catry, P., Costa, H., Elias, G. & Matias, R. (2010). *Aves de Portugal. Ornitologia do território continental.* Assírio & Alvim, Lisboa.

Costa, H. & Comité Português de Raridades da SPEA 1997. Aves de ocorrência rara ou acidental em Portugal. Relatório do Comité Português de Raridades referente ao ano de 1995. *Pardela* 5: 4-19.

Costa, H. & Farinha, J. C. (compil.) 1994. Lista das observações de aves de ocorrência rara ou acidental homologadas pelo Comité Ibérico de Raridades. *Airo* 5: 37-40.

Costa, H. & Farinha, J. C. (compil.) 1995. Lista de observações de aves de ocorrência rara ou acidental em Portugal, homologadas pelo Comité Ibérico de Raridades. *Airo* 6: 76-79.

Costa, H. & Farinha, J. C. (compil.) 1996. Lista das observações de aves de ocorrência rara ou acidental em Portugal homologadas pelo Comité Ibérico de Raridades. *Airo* 7 (2): 96-98.

Costa, H., Bolton, M., Catry, P., Gordinho, L. & Moore, C. C. 1999a. Aves de ocorrência rara ou acidental em Portugal. Relatório do Comité Português de Raridades referente ao ano de 1996. *Pardela* 8: 3-23.

Costa, H., Bolton, M., Catry, P., Matias, R., Moore, C. C. & Tomé, R. 2000b. Aves de ocorrência rara ou acidental em Portugal. Relatório do Comité Português de Raridades referente aos anos de 1997 e 1998. *Pardela* 11: 3-27.

Costa, H., Bolton, M., Matias, R., Moore, C. C. & Tomé, R. 2003. Aves de ocorrência rara ou acidental em Portugal. Relatório do

Comité Português de Raridades referentes aos anos de 1999, 2000 e 2001. *Anuário Ornitológico* 1: 3-35.

Crochet P.-A., Joynt G. (2015). *AERC list of Western Palearctic birds.* July 2015 version. Available at http://www.aerc.eu/tac.html. Viewed 13 March 2016.

Elias, G., Costa, H., Matias, R., Moore, C. C. & Tomé, R. 2004. Aves de ocorrência rara ou acidental em Portugal. Relatório do Comité Português de Raridades referente ao ano de 2002. *Anuário Ornitológico* 2: 1-20.

Elias, G., Costa, H., Matias, R., Moore, C. C. & Tomé, R. 2005. Aves de ocorrência rara ou acidental em Portugal. Relatório do Comité Português de Raridades referente ao ano de 2003. *Anuário Ornitológico* 3: 1-22.

Elias, G., Costa, H., Matias, R., Moore, C. C. & Tomé, R. 2006. Aves de ocorrência rara ou acidental em Portugal. Relatório do Comité Português de Raridades referente ao ano de 2004. *Anuário Ornitológico* 4: 1-16.

Equipa Atlas 2008. *Atlas das Aves Nidificantes em Portugal (1999-2005).* Instituto da Conservação da Natureza, Sociedade Portuguesa para o Estudo das Aves, Parque Natural da Madeira e Secretaria Regional do Ambiente e do Mar. Assírio & Alvim, Lisboa.

Farinha, J. C. & Costa, H. 1993. Lista de observações de aves de ocorrência rara ou acidental em Portugal, homologadas pelo Comité Ibérico de Raridades. *Airo* 4: 34-37.

Farinha, J. C. (Compil.) 1991c. Lista das observações de aves efectuadas em Portugal, aceites pelo Comité Ibérico de Raridades. *Airo* 2: 25-27.

Jara, J., Alfrey, P., Costa, H., Matias, R., Moore, C. C., Santos, J. L. & Tipper, R. Relatório do Comité Português de Raridades referente aos anos de 2008 e 2009. *Anuário Ornitológico* 7: 3-71.

Jara, J., Costa, H., Elias, G., Matias, R., Moore, C.C. & Tomé, R. 2007. Aves de ocorrência rara ou acidental em Portugal. Relatório do Comité Português de Raridades referente ao ano de 2005. *Anuário Ornitológico* 5: 1-34.

Jara, J., Costa, H., Matias, R., Moore, C. C., Noivo, C. & Tipper, R. 2009. Aves de ocorrência rara ou acidental em Portugal. *Anuário Ornitológico* 6: 1-45.

Matias, R. & Lobo, F. 1999. *Aves exóticas que nidificam em Portugal Continental*. Unpublished report. SPEA, Lisboa.

Matias, R. (Comp.) 2003. Aves exóticas em Portugal: anos de 2000 e 2001. *Anuário Ornitológico* 1: 47-51.

Matias, R. (Comp.) 2004. Aves exóticas em Portugal: ano de 2002. *Anuário Ornitológico* 2: 55-63.

Matias, R. (Comp.) 2006a Aves exóticas em Portugal: anos de 2003 e 2004. *Anuário Ornitológico* 4: 55-63.

Matias, R. 2002. *Aves Exóticas que Nidificam em Portugal Continental*. Instituto da Conservação da Natureza, Lisboa.

Matias, R. 2009-10. Aves exóticas em Portugal: anos de 2005-2008. *Anuário Ornitológico* 7: 95-108. Available online at: http://www.spea.pt/fotos/editor2/spea_anuario_ornitologico_a ves_exoticas_em_portugal_2005_2008_p95_108.pdf. Viewed 7 March 2016.

Matias, R. 2011. Aves exóticas em Portugal: anos de 2009 e 2010. *Anuário Ornitológico* 8: 94-104. Available online at: http://www.spea.pt/fotos/editor2/anuario_ornitologico8_3.pdf. Viewed 7 March 2016.

Matias, R., Catry, P., Costa, H., Elias, G., Jara, J, Moore, C.C. & Tomé, R. 2007. Lista sistemática das aves de Portugal Continental. *Anuário Ornitológico* 5: 74-132.

Muchaxo, J., Alfrey, P., Costa, H., Jara, J., Matias, R., Moore, C. C., Santos, J. L. & Tipper, R. Aves de ocorrência rara ou acidental em Portugal. Relatório do Comité Português de Raridades referente ao ano de 2010. *Anuário Ornitológico* 8: 3-52.

Reis Júnior, J. A. 1931. *Catálogo Sistemático e Analítico das Aves de Portugal*. Araújo & Sobrinhos e Sucessores, Porto.

Rufino, R. (Coord.) 1989a. *Atlas das Aves que Nidificam em Portugal Continental*. CEMPA / SNPRCN, Lisboa.

Index

D

E

X

Y

Z

Glossary of place names

The following list contains the names of the places mentioned in the text, along with a short description of their whereabouts. The most important towns, as well as the most prominent capes, are included in the map presented on the following page (Figure 1).

Alcoutim – a small town at the northeastern tip of the Algarve, on the shore of the river Guadiana

Alentejo – a large province in southern Portugal which covers almost all the territory south of the river Tagus, except the Algarve

Alentejo Litoral – the coastal part of the Alentejo province; it is about 50 km wide and extends from the Sado estuary southwards to the Algarve

Algarve – the southernmost province of Portugal, ranging from Cape St. Vincent in the west to Castro Marim in the east

Aljezur – a small town in the northwestern Algarve

Ancão beach – a small beach lying west of Quinta do Lago, in central Algarve

Armação de Pera – a coastal town in the western Algarve, close to Salgados lagoon

Baixo Alentejo – the southern part of the Alentejo, corresponding to the district of Beja, with the exception of the county of Odemira, which is part of the Alentejo Litoral

Barão de São João – a village lying west of Lagos, in the western Algarve

Barranco do Velho – a village lying in the hills of central Algarve, in Loulé county

Barrancos – a small town in the easternmost tip of the Alentejo

Beja – the main town in the southern part of the Alentejo, lying about 100 km north of the Algarve

Boliqueime – a village in central Algarve, just north of Vilamoura

Cape St. Vincent – forms the southwestern tip of the Iberian Peninsula, this is the place where Portugal's south and west coasts meet

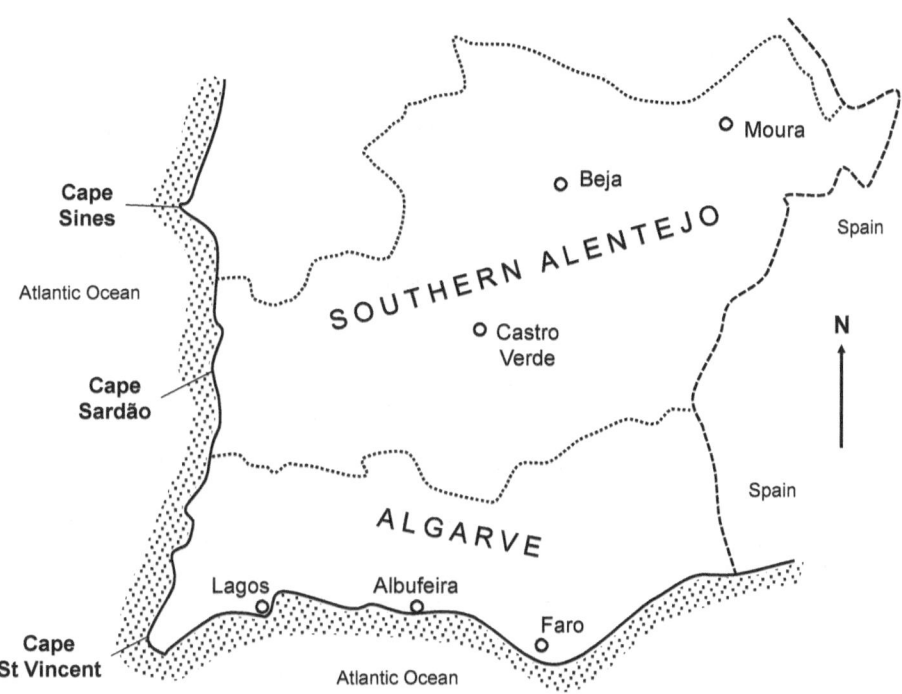

Figure 1 – Map of southern Portugal (Beja and Faro districts),
showing the main towns and the most prominent capes

Castro Marim – a small town in the eastern Algarve, near the mouth of the river Guadiana; it is also the name of a small nature reserve nearby

Castro Verde – a small town in the Baixo Alentejo, which lies in the middle of the plains

Dunas Douradas beach – a small beach just west of Quinta do Lago, in central Algarve

Exclusive Economic Zone – an area of sea stretching from the coastline out to 200 nautical miles from the coast

Faro – the capital city of Algarve, lying close to the south coast in the central part of the province

Ferreira do Alentejo – a small town in the province of Baixo Alentejo, slightly west of its main town, Beja

Fuseta – a coastal village in the eastern Algarve, about 20 km east of Faro

Guadiana – one of the three largest catchments in the country; it runs westwards from Spain and turns south as it approaches Portugal; it reaches the sea near Castro Marim

Lagoa – a small town in the western Algarve, about 50 km west of Faro

Lagoa do Almargem – a small coastal lagoon just east of Quarteira, in central Algarve

Lagoa dos Patos – although it is known as Lagoa (Portuguese for 'lagoon'), this is actually a reservoir; it lies in the middle of the Alentejo, about 30 km northwest of Beja

Ludo – a farm in Ria Formosa, which lies just northwest of Faro airport

Mértola – a small town in sotheastern Alentejo, in the Guadiana river valley

Mexilhoeira Grande – a village near the Ria de Alvor, in the western Algarve

Moura – a town in eastern Alentejo, lying about 40 km east of Beja

Odemira – a small town in southwestern Alentejo

Ponta da Almádena – a cliff west of Lagos, in the western Algarve

Ponta da Atalaia – a cliff on the southwest coast, about 40 km north of Cape St. Vincent

Ponta da Piedade – a large cliff close to the town of Lagos, in the western Algarve

Portimão – a town in the western Algarve, located by the river Arade

Quarteira – a coastal town in central Algarve, lying east of Albufeira

Quinta do Lago – an expensive tourist resort in the central Algarve

Ria de Alvor – a small estuary in the western Algarve, lying between Portimão and Lagos

Ria Formosa – this is the largest wetland in the Algarve, extending over much of the central and eastern Algarve; the widest area lies around Faro

Sagres – a village near Cape St. Vincent, in the western Algarve, near the southwesternmost point in the country

Salgados lagoon – a coastal lagoon in the Algarve, (known as 'Lagoa dos Salgados' in Portuguese), lying slightly west of Albufeira

Santa Luzia (salt pans) – a complex of salt pans near Tavira, eastern Algarve

Serra de Monchique – a chain of hills in the western Algarve, rising to about 900m

Serra do Caldeirão – a chain of hills in central Algarve, forming the border between this province and southern Alentejo

Tavira – a coastal town in the eastern Algarve

Vila do Bispo – a small town near the southwesternmost tip of Portugal, in the western Algarve

Vilamoura – a well-known luxury tourist resort in central Algarve, not far from Quinta do Lago

Vila Nova de Milfontes – a small coastal town in the Alentejo, lying at the Mira river mouth

Vila Real de Santo António – a coastal town lying in the southeastern corner of the Algarvem near the Guadiana river mouth

About the author

Gonçalo Elias was born in Lisbon, Portugal, in 1968. He started watching birds seriously in December 1987. He has wide-ranging field experience and a good knowledge of Portugal's territory, having visited all the counties in the mainland and almost all the islands. He has also explored over 30 different countries in four continents, in order to watch birds and has taken part in eight ornithological atlas projects in Portugal, Spain and Tanzania. He has authored or co-authored eight books about the Portuguese birds and the best places to watch them: *Guia das Aves de Lisboa, As Aves do Estuário do Tejo, Atlas das Aves Invernantes do Baixo Alentejo, A Birdwatcher's Guide to Portugal and Madeira, As Aves do Estuário do Sado, Aves de Portugal – Ornitologia do território continental, Aves de Portugal Continental – Lista Anotada* and *Birds of Portugal – An Annotated Checklist*, along with several papers and notes in specialized journals. He is a founding member of SPEA – Sociedade Portuguesa para o Estudo das Aves, and was a member of the board between 1999 and 2002. He was the coordinator of the Portuguese Rarities Committee between 2002 and 2006. Since 2007 he has been actively promoting birdwatching using the new information and communication technologies; he is a founding member and administrator of Forum Aves (the largest online community of birdwatchers in Portugal), which was launched in July 2007, and also a founding member and coordinator of the avesdeportugal.info website, launched in January 2008. Within the scope of this website, he has been organizing, since 2011, free online courses, aiming at promoting skills in identification of the wild birds occurring in Portugal.

He has a degree in Electrotechnical and Computer Engineering (IST, 1991) and has an MBA (UNL, 1996); additionally, he is a professional trainer, certified by the IEFP.